781 S365c

Schoenberg, Arnold, 1874-
1951.

Coherence, counterpoint,
instrumentation,

DATE DUE

NOV 1 7 1999			
JUL 0 6 2006			
APR 0 6 2008			
DEC 1 8 2009			

DEMCO 38-297

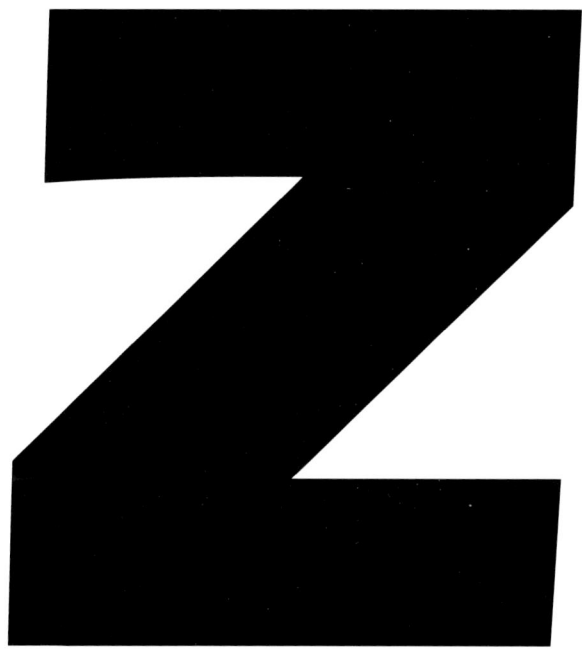

ENTERED
NOV. 1996

Arnold Schoenberg in army uniform, Austria, 1916. Reprinted by arrangement with the Arnold Schoenberg Institute.

Charlie Chaplin, Gertrud and Arnold Schoenberg, and David Raskin, Los Angeles, ca. 1935. Photograph by Max Munn Autrey. Reprinted by arrangement with the Arnold Schoenberg Institute.

*Portrait of Arnold Schoenberg
painted by Max Oppenheimer, 1909.
Reprinted by arrangement with
the Arnold Schoenberg Institute.*

*Alexander Zemlinsky and
Arnold Schoenberg, Prague, 1917.
Photograph by Schlosser Wenisch.
Reprinted by arrangement with
the Arnold Schoenberg Institute.*

"Vision," by Arnold Schoenberg,
oil on cardboard, undated painting.
Reprinted by arrangement with
the Arnold Schoenberg Institute.

ZUSAMMENHANG,
Coherence, Counter-
KONTRAPUNKT,
point, Instrumentation,
INSTRUMENTATION,
Instruction in Form
FORMENLEHRE

by Arnold Schoenberg

Edited and with an introduction by Severine Neff

Translated by Charlotte M. Cross and Severine Neff

University of Nebraska Press: Lincoln and London

© 1994 by the University of Nebraska Press] All rights reserved] Manufactured in the United States of America]

The paper in this book meets the minimum requirements of American National Standard for Information Sciences — Permanence of Paper for Printed Library Materials, ANSI Z39.48-1984.] Library of Congress Cataloging in Publication Data] Schoenberg, Arnold, 1874–1951.] {Zusammenhang, Kontrapunkt, Instrumentation, Formenlehre. English}] Coherence, counterpoint, instrumentation, instruction in form = Zusammenhang, Kontrapunkt, Instrumentation, Formenlehre / by Arnold Schoenberg ; edited and with an introduction by Severine Neff; translated by Charlotte M. Cross and Severine Neff.] p. cm.] Includes bibliographical references and index.] ISBN 0-8032-4230-1 (cl: alkaline paper)] 1. Music — Theory.] 2. Composition (Music)] 3. Instrumentation and orchestration.] I. Neff, Severine, 1949–.] II. Title.] MT6.S316Z913 1993 781—dc20 92-46699 CIP MN

```
781 S365c
Schoenberg, Arnold, 1874-
1951.
Coherence, counterpoint,
instrumentation,
```

IN MEMORY OF ARNOLD SCHOENBERG

Contents

Preface, xix
Acknowledgments, xx
Introduction, xxiii
Note on the Texts, xxi

Coherence, Counterpoint, Instrumentation, Instruction in Form

Foreword, 3
Coherence, 3
Counterpoint, 65
Instrumentation, 77
Instruction in Form, 103

Appendix 1 Schoenberg's Indexes, 109

Appendix 2 A Table of Contents for Each Notebook of ZKIF, 119

Appendix 3 Two Bibliographic Lists Compiled by Schoenberg, 121

Appendix 4 A Comparison of Schoenberg's Lists and Rufer's Catalogue, 125

Appendix 5 A Comparison of Christensen and Christensen with Rufer and with Schoenberg, 129

Works Cited, 131
Index, 133

Preface

This volume presents a transcription and translation of Arnold Schoenberg's incomplete theoretical manuscript "Zusammenhang, Kontrapunkt, Instrumentation, Formenlehre" {Coherence, Counterpoint, Instrumentation, Instruction in Form}, henceforth referred to as ZKIF. Begun in April 1917, during Schoenberg's early attempts at formulating the twelve-tone method, this seventy-five-page text was the composer's most lengthy theoretical work since the completion of the *Harmonielehre* in 1911 and his most ambitious theoretical work until the writing of the 150-page manuscript "Der musikalische Gedanke und die Logik, Technik und Kunst seiner Darstellung {The musical idea and the logic, technique, and art of its presentation} in 1934–36. The manuscript itself constituted the beginnings of four books: while the projected books on counterpoint, instrumentation, and form were to be practical manuals, Schoenberg intended the text on coherence to present a theory that would unify the separate disciplines of counterpoint, instrumentation, form, and harmony. Several years later, in 1923, Schoenberg's thoughts on the nature of coherence led him to formulate his concept of the "musical idea," which ultimately replaced coherence as the basis of his unified theory.

The book projects of 1917 occupied Schoenberg throughout the course of his life. He continued work on "Counterpoint" in 1926, 1934, and 1936; "Instruction in Form" in 1923 and 1924, and from 1937 to 1948; and "Instrumentation" from 1945 until his death, in 1951. He also wrote various essays on the "musical idea" that extend his ideas of coherence, the most crucial being the above-mentioned "Der musikalische Gedanke und die Logik, Technik und Kunst seiner Darstellung." As early as 1923 Schoenberg added a further text on the theory of performance, and around 1925 he decided to write a second book on harmony. Despite Schoenberg's continuing work on these book projects, at the time of his death all remained unfinished. The text of ZKIF is especially fragmentary, consisting essentially of Schoenberg's notes to himself.

Although Schoenberg abandoned the text of ZKIF, he undoubtedly referred to it when writing later essays. The manuscript contains many underlinings in colored pencil that were obviously added through multiple readings; moreover, carbon copies of certain pages were bound with later works; musical examples, too, paralleled those of subsequent essays. Because it served as a source book from which Schoenberg repeatedly borrowed, ZKIF assumes a large role in interpreting the composer's later theoretical writings: a single cryptic sentence in this manuscript in conjunction with a later passage can vividly illumine Schoenberg's thought and reveal the genesis of such crucial ideas as developing variation and liquidation. Thus, the fragmentary text of ZKIF can aid a reader in comprehending Schoenberg's theoretical works as a coherent body of musical thought.

Schoenberg realized that the fragmentary nature of ZKIF made it difficult to use, even for himself: his last addition to each notebook housing the text was an index complete with page numbers. This volume presents ZKIF in the order of Schoenberg's indexes, which group together similar material, thus clarifying the basic ideas of this incomplete work: first we find detailed outlines of the four book projects; then discussions of the nature of coherence and comprehensibility; definitions of motive, rhythm, and the principles of structure; and finally, thoughts on the capabilities and characters of instruments. The original order of the material is preserved in Appendix 2. Later works of Schoenberg, cited in editorial footnotes, clarify obscure references while offering the reader an opportunity to trace the development of the composer's ideas from their genesis in this fragmentary source.

ACKNOWLEDGMENTS

The editor would like to express her deep appreciation to the following persons, without whom this volume could never have taken form.

Above all, the editor gratefully acknowledges the generous support and interest of Nuria Schoenberg Nono and Lawrence and Ronald Schoenberg, who granted her permission to publish this text. Dr. Leonard Stein, Director of the Arnold Schoenberg Institute, remained a source of inspiration and encouragement throughout the project. R. Wayne Shoaf, Archivist of the Arnold Schoenberg Institute, offered expert advice particularly on dating portions of the manuscript.

I would also like to thank my co-translator, Dr. Charlotte M. Cross, for her initial translations of the manuscript, which served as points of departure for subsequent work. Charlotte and I revised the initial translation in part with the helpful suggestions of Professor Thomas Kovach of the University of Utah. In connection with my further reworkings of the text, I would like to thank Professor Patricia Carpenter of Barnard College, a longtime student of Schoenberg, and the German-born harpist Dr. Jasmin Bey Cowin. Dr. Cowin also checked the transcription of the text by Anita Luginbühl housed at the Arnold Schoenberg Institute, Los Angeles. Finally, Charlotte and I wish to thank Professor Claudio Spies of Princeton University for looking over our finished translation with his expert's eye, offering elegant translations of certain passages that remained problematic to the end.

The editor would also like to acknowledge the suggestions of Professor Patricia Carpenter, Professor Joel Feigin, Professor Ethan Haimo, Mr. Christopher Hatch, and Professor Claudio Spies concerning the introduction to the text.

Special thanks also go to Joel Feigin and Mollie and Irwin Feigin and to Victor and Evangeline Neff for their love and support.

Introduction

Upon publication of the *Harmonielehre* in 1911, Arnold Schoenberg wrote to his publisher Emil Hertzka at Universal Edition:

> I would perhaps be ready to draw up a contract for my *entire activities* [italics added] as a writer on music. I plan in the near future the following writings (in addition to the counterpoint [book]):[1] an *instrumentation* text. There is nothing like this now, for all available books deal with the instruments themselves. I wish to teach the art of *composing for orchestra!!* This is a major distinction and something *absolutely new!!*
>
> Then a *Preliminary Study of Form: An Investigation into the formal causes of the effects of modern compositions*. This writing will probably be limited to the study of *Mahler's* works. Then, later also as a preliminary to the study of form, *Formal Analysis and laws resulting from it*. Finally, *Theory of Form*.
>
> All of these books are texts or teaching aids. They form in their entirety an *Aesthetic of Music*, under which title I wish to write a . . . comprehensive work. For all of these works I already have ideas and also notes. I can finish all of them in the course of five years![2]

Not until six years later, however, in April 1917, while lecturing at Dr.

---

1. Schoenberg is referring to the unfinished text "Komposition mit selbständigen Stimmen" (Composition with independent voices), which he began outlining in 1911. For a description of the manuscript, see Josef Rufer, *The Works of Arnold Schoenberg*, trans. Dika Newlin (London: Faber, 1962), 135. For an edition of the text, see Rudolf Stephan, "Schönbergs Entwurf über Das Komposition mit selbständigen Stimmen," *Archiv für Musikwissenschaft* 29 (1972): 239–56.

2. Letter translated in Bryan R. Simms, "Review of *Theory of Harmony* by Arnold Schoenberg, translated by Roy E. Carter," *Music Theory Spectrum* 4 (1982): 156–57.

Eugenie Schwarzwald's school and completing the libretto to *Die Jakobsleiter*,³ did Schoenberg begin working simultaneously on the instrumentation and form books, as well as on a counterpoint book distinct from "Komposition mit selbständigen Stimmen," which he had referred to in his letter to Hertzka. At the same time, he also began work on a newly conceived book on musical coherence (rather than aesthetics). His notes on all four projects are contained in the unpublished manuscript "Zusammenhang, Kontrapunkt, Instrumentation, Formenlehre" [Coherence, counterpoint, instrumentation, instruction in form].⁴ The four topics of ZKIF proved seminal for the major theoretical works of Schoenberg's later life: "Zusammenhang" for the book-length manuscript "Der musikalische Gedanke und die Logik, Technik und Kunst seiner Darstellung" [The musical idea and the logic, technique, and art of its presentation]; "Kontrapunkt" for *Preliminary Exercises in Counterpoint*;⁵ "Instrumentation" for the incomplete manuscript "Theory of Orchestration";⁶ and "Formenlehre" for *Fundamentals of Musical Composition*.⁷ Thus, a study of ZKIF is crucial for understanding

---

3. See letter to Albertine Zehme dated May 5, 1917, in Arnold Schoenberg, *Letters*, ed. Erwin Stein, trans. Eithne Wilkins and Ernst Kaiser (New York: St. Martin's Press, 1965), 53. For information on Schoenberg's lectures for Schwarzwald, a renowned reformer of educational practice, see H. H. Stuckenschmidt, *Schoenberg: His Life, World, and Work*, trans. Humphrey Searle (New York: Schirmer Books, 1977), 245. Stuckenschmidt sees in Schoenberg's lectures the composer's motivation for writing pedagogical texts.

4. Henceforth referred to as ZKIF: for a description of the manuscript, see Rufer, *Works*, 136–37. For a specific reference to book projects, see 3.

5. See Arnold Schoenberg, *The Musical Idea and the Logic, Technique, and Art of Its Presentation*, ed. and trans. Patricia Carpenter and Severine Neff (New York: Columbia University Press, 1994); Arnold Schoenberg, "Der musikalische Gedanke und die Logik, Technik und Kunst seiner Darstellung," manuscript no. T65.1–4 at the Arnold Schoenberg Institute, Los Angeles and catalogued as 3c in Rufer, *Works*, 137; Arnold Schoenberg, *Preliminary Exercises in Counterpoint*, ed. Leonard Stein (New York: St. Martin's Press, 1964).

6. For a description of the manuscript, see Rufer, *Works*, 139; and Jean Christensen and Jesper Christensen, *From Schoenberg's Literary Legacy: A Catalog of Neglected Items* (Warren, Mich.: Harmonie Park Press, 1988), 101–7.

7. Arnold Schoenberg, *Fundamentals of Musical Composition*, ed. Gerald Strang (New York: St. Martin's Press, 1967). Aspects of *Fundamentals of Musical Composition* are also derived from "Der musikalische Gedanke und die Logik, Technik und Kunst seiner Darstellung," e.g., the comparison of theme and melody, and the descriptions of motive, basic motive, phrase, condensation, and liquidation.

the development of Schoenberg's thought. The first major theoretical work written after the *Harmonielehre*, ZKIF contains Schoenberg's first discussion of the technique he called *developing variation*, here illumined by a passage from Mozart's "Dissonant" Quartet, K.465. This explication, Schoenberg's first extended prose analysis, is one of the most precise illustrations of that technique in all his literary works, published or unpublished.

ZKIF exemplifies a major feature of Schoenberg's lifework: the correspondence of significant theoretical activity with crucial turning points in his compositional development. ZKIF was written during the composition of *Die Jakobsleiter*, in which Schoenberg first used a single hexachord as the principal source of motives and themes, a critical concept with respect to the development of serial thinking. Similarly, the *Harmonielehre* (1911) was conceived during the move to atonality, and "Der musikalische Gedanke und die Logik, Technik und Kunst seiner Darstellung" (1934–36) at a time when, owing to the dim prospects of having his twelve-tone works performed, he reverted to tonality for certain compositions.[8] Moreover, 1923, the year Schoenberg announced the twelve-tone method, saw an extraordinary outpouring of short prose works on theory.[9] ZKIF, then, is only one of a series of works Schoenberg wrote during periods of compositional crisis.

Imbuing ZKIF with a tremendous additional importance are the examples for "Kontrapunkt" that contain combinatorial hexachordal studies — examples that must have been written considerably later than 1917. This conclusion is supported by the inclusion in the studies of what is clearly an early, previously unknown sketch for the Variations for Orchestra, op.31, written in 1926. The issues raised by the hexachordal examples must be dealt with thoroughly, and they form the topic of the second part of this introduction, after the initial discussion of the manuscript. Finally, the third part of this essay focuses on theoretical and historical issues.

---

8. The Suite for String Orchestra, completed in 1934, was his first tonal piece of major scope since the first three movements of the String Quartet No. 2 in F♯ Minor, op.10 (1907–8). Two minor works written in the intervening years are also tonal: *Der deutsche Michel* (1914–15) and *Die eiserne Brigade* (1916).

9. See Christensen and Christensen, *Literary Legacy*, 111–14.

HISTORICAL BACKGROUND

A Description of ZKIF

Schoenberg wrote most or all of the seventy-five pages of prose text that make up ZKIF in Mödling, Austria, over a period of thirteen days: April 11–23, 1917.[10] The text is housed in two notebooks, which Schoenberg himself classified under the heading "Unfinished Theoretical Works."[11] The notebook marked "Heft I" (Notebook I) also contains a separate, undated section of musical examples for "Kontrapunkt."[12] The manuscripts can be described as in Table 1.

Table 1. Description of the Manuscripts

NOTEBOOK I

a. Title: "Zusammenhang, Kontrapunkt, Instrumentation, Formenlehre" {Coherence, counterpoint, instrumentation, instruction in form}, Heft I

Dates: April 11, 13–18, 22–23, 1917

Classification: Schoenberg: "Unfinished Theoretical Works," nos. 8–10
Rufer: A-2, p. 136
Arnold Schoenberg Institute: T37.17

Size: 7¼" x 4½"

Number of Pages: 36

Script: Sütterlin; interspersed Roman words and titles

---

10. These dates conform to those on the manuscript. It seems likely that some of the undated portions were actually written in early May. In his letter to Zehme dated May 5, 1917 (see note 3), Schoenberg says he is at work on ZKIF.

11. The sheet on which Schoenberg entered this list is catalogued as T37.1 at the Arnold Schoenberg Institute, Los Angeles. Rufer used the list to compile his chapter "Theoretical Works": see Rufer, *Works*, 133–39. The Christensens seem unaware of its existence (see Christensen and Christensen, *Literary Legacy*, 137, asterisked footnote).

12. On the sheet "Unfinished Theoretical Works," Schoenberg classifies the examples for ZKIF with the material in the first notebook.

Table 1. *Continued*

Medium: lead and lavender pencil; annotations and underlinings in lavender, red, blue, purple, yellow, and lead pencil

b. Title: "Notenbeispiele zu Kontrapunkt, Formenlehre, Instrumentation u. Zusammenhang" {Examples for counterpoint, instruction in form, instrumentation, and coherence}

Dates: undated

Classification: Schoenberg: "Unfinished Theoretical Works," no.8
Rufer: not mentioned in description in A-2, p.136
Arnold Schoenberg Institute: T37.18

Size: 7½" x 11¼"

Number of Pages: 19

Script: Roman and Sütterlin

Medium: lead pencil and red ink

NOTEBOOK II

Title:	A, D, E	Instru.lehre {A, D, E Instruction in instrumentation}
	B	Aufg. Instru.lehre {B Exercises, instruction in instrumentation}
	C	Formenlehre {Instruction in form}
	F, G, H	Zusammenhang {Coherence}

Date: April 18–21, 1917

Classification: Schoenberg: "Unfinished Theoretical Works," no.8
Rufer: A-2, p.136
Arnold Schoenberg Institute: T37.19

Size: 7¼" x 6"

Number of Pages: 39

Script: Sütterlin; interspersed Roman words and titles

Medium: lead pencil; annotations in blue, red, lavender pencil and black crayon and ink

ZKIF consists of a series of notes that Schoenberg jotted down for his own use. He started with "Zusammenhang," the "new" topic unmentioned in the 1911 letter to Hertzka, from which he envisioned his work on the previously projected topics; indeed, at the end of the manuscript he returned again to sections of "Zusammenhang," as can be seen in Table 2. One of Schoenberg's last additions to the manuscript was the inclusion of two indexes, one for each notebook.[13] Each index consists of two sections, general and alphabetical. The general indexes divide the manuscript into material for the four books, while the alphabetical indexes make reference to more detailed topics.

ZKIF is presented here in four discrete sections corresponding to each book project. The sections are compiled from page groupings articulated in Schoenberg's general indexes.[14] The excerpts from "Zusammenhang" are then internally ordered according to the three largest topics mentioned in Schoenberg's alphabetical index: coherence and comprehensibility, motive and rhythm, and principles of structure. Schoenberg's outline for the text begins the section. "Instrumentation" follows an analogous framework: book outline, capabilities and character of instruments, transposition, and exercises. The few topics for "Kontrapunkt" and "Formenlehre" appear in the order in which they were written.

ZKIF *and Schoenberg's Other Theoretical Works*

The influence of ZKIF on Schoenberg's entire theoretical output is made clear only by examining Schoenberg's extant manuscripts and their classifications. Four classification systems exist for Schoenberg's extant literary manuscripts: those of Schoenberg himself, his student Josef Rufer, the musicologists Jean and Jesper Christensen, and the present archivist of the Arnold Schoenberg Institute, R. Wayne Shoaf.[15] Shoaf and the

---

13. The indexes appear in Appendix 1.

14. For example, in his general index Schoenberg lists as belonging to "Zusammenhang" pages 1, 4–5, 6–22, 27–31, and 33–36 in Notebook I and pages 21–22, 29, and 49 {*sic*} in Notebook II (see Appendix 1). The material on these pages appears in the present volume grouped together under the title "Zusammenhang." The presentation of material from the texts of "Kontrapunkt," "Instrumentation," and "Formenlehre" follow an analogous procedure. The original order of excerpts in ZKIF is presented in Appendix 2.

15. See Christensen and Christensen, *Literary Legacy*, and Rufer, *Works*. Schoenberg's major catalogues appear in Christensen and Christensen, *Literary Legacy*, 109–38.

Table 2. The Chronology of ZKIF

Date	Page[a]	Book
11/IV.17	I:2–4	Z and K[b]
	I:5–7	Z
13/IV.17	I:7–16	Z
14/IV.17	I:16	K
	I:16–18	Z
15/IV.17	I:23–24	I
16/IV.17	I:20–22	Z
	I:25	I
17/IV.17	I:18–19, 28	Z
	I:27	F
18/IV.17	I:28–32	Z
	II:1–2	I
19/IV.17	II:3–5	I
20/IV.17	I:27	F
	I:32	K, I[c]
	II:7, 9	I
	II:10–11	F
21/IV.17	II:12–16, 18–19	I
	II:21–22	Z
22/IV.17	I:33	Z
23/IV.17	I:33–36	Z
undated	I:1	Z
	II:29–30	Z
	mus. ex.	K
	II:35–38, 49 {sic}	Z

a. "I" refers to Notebook I, "II" to Notebook II

b. Parts of the manuscript Schoenberg catalogued as belonging to both "Zusammenhang" and "Kontrapunkt."

c. These are discrete units of "Kontrapunkt" and "Instrumentation."

former archivist Jerry McBride made the decision to abandon the first ordering of the institute's materials, an inventory compiled by the original archivist, Clara Steuermann, and her assistants. As archivist, Shoaf then imposed Schoenberg's original orderings on the manuscripts and subsequently assigned catalogue numbers to them.[16]

Schoenberg himself made two master lists and three partial lists of his literary manuscripts. Fearing that his imminent flight from Germany would result in a loss of those manuscripts, on June 2, 1932, he began the first such list; it was completed after 1940.[17] His usual manner of classification was to place the sheets in chronological order, stamp them with a number, and give them a subject category. Certain manuscripts on this list, however, remain undated; others are cross-referenced. As he listed, Schoenberg added short commentaries, stylistic revisions, titles, and subject headings.

The subject categories assigned to the manuscripts in the first list succinctly illustrate Schoenberg's intellectual concerns. The chart in Table 3 summarizes Schoenberg's categories and his abbreviations of them. "Musikalisches" is the largest category; "Anekdoten" and "Natur" hardly materialized. In 1933 Schoenberg considered adding the category "Jude" [Jew] for his writings on Jewish concerns.[18]

After 1940 Schoenberg continued his bibliographic work with a second inventory, entitled "List of the Manuscripts, Mostly Handwritten, of Articles, Essays, Outlines, Sketches, Notes, Critical Remarks and Fragments," which contains entries in typescript, in Schoenberg's hand, and in another, unidentified hand.[19] Here Schoenberg describes each work according to number, title, and possible date. The contents of the entry "Kleine Manuscripte I and II" are further described in two addenda at the conclusion of the second main list of manuscripts.

A third addendum, unrelated to the contents of "Kleine Manuscripte

---

16. Letter to Severine Neff from R. Wayne Shoaf, February 2, 1989.

17. For a documented description of these events, see Christensen and Christensen, *Literary Legacy*, 4.

18. See Christensen and Christensen, *Literary Legacy*, 6. Schoenberg's complete description of his categories, with extended subtitles, appears in ibid., Appendix 1, and a complete transcription of the initial catalogue appears in ibid., Appendix 2, pp. 109–29. DENK 202 and 301 also have the secondary category "Pranger" {Pillory}: perhaps Schoenberg wished to punish the persons mentioned in his commentary.

19. A transcription of the entire list appears in ibid., Appendix 3, pp. 131–38.

Table 3. Subject Categories in Schoenberg's First Main List

1.	Aesthetik	(Aesthetics)	[Kü]
2.	Anekdoten	(Anecdotes)	[An]
3.	Aphorismen	(Aphorisms)	[Aph]
4.	Biographisches	(Biographical)	[Bio]
5.	Denkmäler	(Monuments)	[Denk]
6.	Meine Theorien	(My theories)	[Deut]
7.	Moral	(Ethics)	[Mor]
8.	Musikalisches	(Musical)	[Mus]
9.	Natur	(Nature)	
	Physik	(Physics)	
	Tiere	(Animals)	[Nat]
10.	Sprachliches	(Linguistic)	[Spr]
11.	Vermischtes	(Miscellaneous)	[Verm]

1 and 11," was begun. Its initial citation corresponds to entry no.2 on a different, more complete typed list, "Unfinished Theoretical Works" (see Appendix III in the present volume). It is in the latter list that ZKIF is catalogued. Yet another list, "*Manuscripts*, Mostly (Real Manuscripts) Handwritten, Some Perhaps Unpublished, Some Fragments," enumerates several other theoretical manuscripts.[20] A transcription of this sheet also appears in Appendix 3. A final list, "Gedruckte Aufsätze" [Published articles] includes theoretical commentaries, such as Schoenberg's analysis of his String Quartet No.1, op.7.[21]

---

20. This sheet is catalogued at the Arnold Schoenberg Institute under the manuscript no. T20.1. "*Manuscripts,* Mostly (Real Manuscripts) Handwritten," "Unfinished Theoretical Works," and "List of the Manuscripts" appear to have been prepared on the same typewriter.

21. For a facsimile of the list, entitled "Gedruckte Artikel {*sic*}," see Walter B. Bailey, "Schoenberg's Published Articles: A List of Titles, Sources, and Translations," *Journal of the Arnold Schoenberg Institute* 4, no.2 (1980): 158–59.

In 1957 a student of Schoenberg's, the composer Joseph Rufer, began to put together a catalogue of Schoenberg's musical and literary works. Rufer's groupings of prose manuscripts are in part compilations of discrete subject categories in Schoenberg's 1932–40 list.[22] Rufer altered Schoenberg's system in several ways, however, and his lists are incomplete. For example, Schoenberg's earliest "Gedanke" manuscript, mentioned in his 1932–40 list as "MUS 56," does not appear anywhere. Rufer also omits the entire contents of the categories "Biographisches," "Anekdoten," and "Natur, Physik, Tiere," and almost all of "Aphorismen." Rufer's section "Articles, Essays" (156–60) does correspond to nos. 1–141 in Schoenberg's list, but a portion of it also includes late manuscripts in English that Schoenberg himself failed to catalogue, as well as certain entries from Schoenberg's list "Unfinished Theoretical Works." The remaining entries on that sheet, including the manuscript ZKIF, appear in Rufer's chapter "Theoretical Works" (133–51). The chart in Appendix 4 offers a comparative summary of Schoenberg's lists and Rufer's catalogue.

In a few cases only Rufer's catalogue contains readily accessible information concerning the physical grouping of manuscripts by Schoenberg himself. This information is particularly significant with respect to ZKIF. For example, Rufer describes two carbon copies of the section "Verstehen = Erkennen der Ähnlichkeit" [Understanding: Recognition of similarity] from "Zusammenhang," one bound with "Komposition mit selbständigen Stimmen" (1911), and the other with a later manuscript on the musical idea (136–37). Both appended carbon copies are now apparently lost.[23] In this light, Rufer's catalogue is the only source showing such interconnections between ZKIF and other works.

The 1988 catalogue by Jean and Jesper Christensen, *From Schoenberg's Literary Legacy: A Catalog of Neglected Items*, is a major contribution to Schoenberg bibliography. It gives detailed descriptions for each entry under Schoenberg's subject categories, including the categories that are omitted either entirely or in part by Rufer. The Christensens also give detailed descriptions of manuscript categories that they them-

---

22. See Rufer, *Works*, 164–69. Page numbers cited in this paragraph and the next refer to this text.

23. Shoaf confirms this point in his letter of February 2, 1989.

selves have construed, the entries for which remain unlisted in Schoenberg and uncatalogued by Rufer.[24] Appendix 5 compares the Christensens's catalogue with that of Rufer and with Schoenberg's lists.

Schoenberg's lists, in conjunction with the work of Rufer, the Christensens, and the archivists of the Arnold Schoenberg Institute, make it possible for the first time to see chronologically all the published and unpublished theoretical manuscripts. Moreover, Schoenberg's classifications of his manuscripts allow for groupings according to their subject matter. Schoenberg classifies most of his theoretical works under the descriptive category "Musical." Others, such as ZKIF, appear on the sheet "Unfinished Theoretical Works." When grouped according to their specific subject matter, the overwhelming majority of theoretical manuscripts fall into the four major topics of ZKIF: coherence, counterpoint, orchestration, and form. The remaining theoretical manuscripts clearly fall either into the topics of three late texts on performance, harmony, and the twelve-tone method, or into essays and comments on the "musical idea," which frequently continue or develop certain ideas set forth in "Coherence." Schoenberg intended the "idea" manuscripts to be part of a book, *Kompositionslehre*. These groupings, as set forth in Tables 4 and 5, thus demonstrate the significance of ZKIF as a seed of Schoenberg's theoretical works.

On the one hand, portions of ZKIF bear direct correspondence to later works within their respective groupings. Schoenberg's writings on coherence led into a much larger body of works on the "musical idea." For example, the analysis of Mozart's "Dissonant" Quartet, K.465, begun in ZKIF, is continued and elaborated in "Der musikalische Gedanke und die Logik, Technik und Kunst seiner Darstellung" (1934–36).[25] On the other hand, the undated hexachordal examples in "Kontrapunkt" are unique; in fact, they have major historical significance, the least of which is that they contain the only nontonal procedures dealt with in any text on counterpoint. These curious examples deserve detailed scrutiny.

---

24. Christensen and Christensen, *Literary Legacy*, 12.

25. See Schoenberg, "Der musikalische Gedanke und die Logik, Technik und Kunst seiner Darstellung," 34a.

Table 4. A Chronology of Theoretical Works Dealing with the Four Topics in ZKIF

Schoenberg's manuscript classification appears in brackets after each title for which he provided one. Proposed texts are followed by the symbol [P] and appropriate reference. Published manuscripts have the following abbreviated references: SI = *Style and Idea*, L = *Letters*; PEC = *Preliminary Exercises in Counterpoint*.

Coherence

1917	"Zusammenhang" (Coherence), in ZKIF ["Unfinished Theoretical Works," no.8]
1922	"Lehre vom musikalischen Zusammenhang" (Theory of musical coherence) [P], [L, 71]
1923	"Gelehrsamkeit" (Erudition)[a] [Mus 28]

Counterpoint

1911	"Komposition mit selbständigen Stimmen" (Composition with independent voices), also catalogued by Schoenberg as "Outlines of Theories: Counterpoint, Instrumentation" ["Unfinished Theoretical Works," no.2]
1917	"Kontrapunkt" (Counterpoint), in ZKIF ["Unfinished Theoretical Works," no.8]
1924	"Theorie der mehrstimmigen (kontrapuntischen) Komposition" (Theory of polyphonic {contrapuntal} composition) [P] [SI, 23–24]
1926	"Kontrapunkt" (Counterpoint) ["Unfinished Theoretical Works," no.4]
1929	"Disposition eines Lehrbuchs des Kontrapunkts" (Layout of a textbook on counterpoint) [P] [Mus 165][b]
1934	"Preface and Introduction to the Counterpoint Textbook" ["*Manuscripts*, Mostly (Real Manuscripts) Handwritten, etc.," no.8]

Table 4. *Continued*

1936	"Counterpoint" ["Unfinished Theoretical Works," no.5] [PEC, 121–22]
1942–43	Untitled[c] [no. I-d in Rufer, *Works*, 136]
1964	*Preliminary Exercises in Counterpoint*, ed. Leonard Stein. New York: St. Martin's Press, 1964

Addenda: The following articles address issues in the above attempts at writing a counterpoint text. Their specific relation to any book, however, remains unclear.

1923	"Mißverständnis des Kontrapunkts" (Misunderstandings of counterpoint) [Mus 46b]
	"Polyphonie-Heute" (Polyphony today) [Mus 40]
1924	"Gratulation an Bach" (Congratulations to Bach) [Mus 147]
	"Fuga-Flucht" (Fugue flight) [Mus 78a/Spr 78b]
1926?	"Durchführung" (Elaboration) [Mor 177a/Mus 177b]
1927	"Kontrapunkt" (Counterpoint) [Aph 228]
1928	"Zu Werkers Bach-Studien" (On Werker's study of Bach)[d]
	"Alter und neuer Kontrapunkt" (Old and new counterpoint) [SI, 288–89]
1928?	"Linearer Kontrapunkt, Lineare Polyphonie" (Linear counterpoint, linear polyphony) [SI, 295–97]
1928/1929	"Herr Urban (Berliner Zeitung)" (Mr. Urban {Berlin newspaper}) [Denk 346]
1931	"Der lineare Kontrapunkt" (Linear counterpoint) [SI, 289–95]
1932	"Bach und die 12 Töne" (Bach and the twelve tones) [Mus 214]

Table 4. *Continued*

	"Zwei sehr wichtige Definitionen a) RHYTHMUS b) KONTRAPUNKT" (Two very important definitions a) RHYTHM b) COUNTERPOINT) [Mus 394]
1936	"Der Fuge ist . . ." (The fugue is . . .) [SI, 297–98]
1950	"Bach" [SI, 393–97]
post-1945	"Bach's Counterpoint" [no. C-191 in Rufer, *Works*, 162]
	"Something about Bach" [no. C-229b in Rufer, *Works*, 164]
undated	"Counterpoint in the Nineteenth and Twentieth Centuries" [no. D-112 in Rufer, *Works*, 108]

Orchestration

1911	"Outline of Theories: Counterpoint, Instrumentation" ["Unfinished Theoretical Works," no.2]
between 1916 and 1918	Notizen zu Klavier-Auszug (Notes on Piano Reduction) [MUS 383]
1917	"Instrumentation" (Instrumentation) in ZKIF ["Unfinished Theoretical Works," nos.8–11]
1923	"Transposition" (Transposition) [SI, 343–45]
1923	"Über Klavierauszug" (On the piano reduction) [SI, 348–50]
1924	"Jens Quer über: Das Orchester der Zukunft" (Jens Quer on the orchestra of the future) [SI, 322–25]
1926	"Mechanische Musikinstrumente" (Mechanical musical instruments) [SI, 326–30]
1931	"Instrumentation" (Instrumentation) [Mus 171]

Table 4. *Continued*

1949	"Various Titled and Untitled Works" [Christensen and Christensen, *Literary Legacy*, "Orchestration," 101–7]
Form	
1917	"Formenlehre" (Instruction in form), in ZKIF ["Unfinished Theoretical Works," no.8]
1917	"Mahlers IX. Symphonie" (Mahler's Ninth Symphony) [P] ["Unfinished Theoretical Works," no.12]
1923	"Zur Terminologie der Formenlehre" (On the terminology for the instruction in form) [Mus 66a–c]
1924	"Formenlehre" (Instruction in form) [SI, 253–55]
1925	"Tonalität und Gliederung" (Tonality and articulation) [SI, 255–57]
1928	"Die alten Formen in neuen Musik" (Old forms in new music) [Mus 159]
1938	"The Concept of Form" [Mus 352]
c. 1938	"Symphonische Form" (Symphonic form) [Mus 373]
undated	"Zu Formenlehre" (On the theory of form) [Mus 335]
1942	*Models for Beginners in Composition*, New York: G. Schirmer, 1942
1947	Notebook with notes on form [no. C-185 in Rufer, *Works*, 162]
post-1945	"Form" [no. C-180 in Rufer, *Works*, 162]
	"Tonality" [no. C-179 in Rufer, *Works*, 161]
undated	"Zur Formenlehre" (On the Theory of Form) [no.21, "List of the Manuscripts"]
	"The term scherzo . . ." [Christensen and Christensen, *Literary Legacy*, "Notebooks," 1-7, 96]

Table 4. *Continued*

1937–48	*Fundamentals of Musical Composition*, ed. Gerald Strang, New York: St. Martin's Press, 1967

[a]Schoenberg indicates that this manuscript is part of "Lehre vom musikalischen Zusammenhang."

[b]Rufer mistakenly dates this manuscript as 1931: see no. D-67 in Rufer, *Works*, 166.

[c]This entry, consisting of extensive notes and drafts, is the main source of the posthumously published text *Preliminary Exercises in Counterpoint* (1964).

[d]Leonard Stein, "Schoenberg: Five Statements," *Perspectives of New Music* 14, no.1 (1975): 168–71.

Table 5. A Chronology of the "Kompositionslehre" and the Performance, Harmony, and Twelve-Tone Texts[a]

Theory of Composition

1923	"Zu Darstellung des Gedankens" (On the presentation of the idea) [Mus 56]
1924	"Die Gesetze der musikalischen Komposition" (The laws of musical composition) [P] [SI, 23–24]
1925	"Kompositionslehre: Der musikalische Gedanke, seine Darstellung und Durchführung" (Theory of composition: The musical idea, its presentation and elaboration). Short title: "Gedanke und Darstellung" (Idea and presentation) ["Unfinished Theoretical Works," no.3, Ba]
1928–33	"Der Gedanke und die Zange" (The idea and pliers) [Verm 341]
undated, 1929, 1940	"Kompositionslehre: Der musikalische Gedanke und seine Darstellung" (Theory of composition: The musical idea and its presentation) ["Unfinished Theoretical Works," no.3, Bb]
1930?	"Zur Kompositionslehre" (On the theory of composition) [SI, 264–68]

Table 5. *Continued*

c. 1930	"Neue Musik, Meine Musik" (New music, my music) [SI, 99–106]
1931	"Zu: Darstellung des musikalischen Gedankens" (On the presentation of the musical idea) [Mus 275a/b]
1931	"Entwurf zum Vorwort des Kompositionslehre" (Sketch for a preface to the theory of composition) [Mus 276]
1932	"Zu: Darstellung des Gedankens" (On the presentation of the musical idea) [Rufer, *Works*, 140]
1934	"The Musical Idea" ["Manuscripts, Mostly (Real Manuscripts) Handwritten," no.9]
1934–36	"Der musikalische Gedanke und die Logik, Technik und Kunst seiner Darstellung" (The musical idea and the logic, technique, and art of its presentation) [no. A-3c in Rufer, *Works*, 137–38]
1930/46	"New Music, Outmoded Music, Style, and Idea" [SI, 113–24]
c. 1948	"Connection of Musical Ideas" [SI, 287–88]
1940	"Fragmente" (Fragments) [Christensen and Christensen, *Literary Legacy*, "Fragmente" III-1-A, 5-D, 41–42]
undated	"Der musikalische Gedanke; seine Darstellung und Durchfuehrung" (The musical idea: Its presentation and elaboration) ["Unfinished Theoretical Works," no.3, Aa]
undated	"Gedanke" (Idea) ["Unfinished Theoretical Works," Ab]

Performance

1923	"Vortragszeichen" (Performance indications) [SI, 340]
1923	"Bogen" (Slurs) [Mus 47]
1923	"Ich sehe mit Schrecken . . ." (I note with alarm . . .) [Christensen and Christensen, *Literary Legacy*, "Kleine Manuskripte," II-15, 55.]
1923	"Noten-Bilder-Schrift" (Pictorial notation) [SI, 351–52]

Table 5. *Continued*

1923?	"Zur Vortragslehre" (For the treatise on performance) [SI, 319–20]
1924	"Eine Neue Zwölfton-Schrift" (A new twelve-tone notation) [SI, 354–62]
1926	"Zur Metronomisierung" (On metronome markings) [SI, 342]
1926	"Zur Metronomisierung" (On metronome markings) [Mus 138]
1926	"Zur Metronomisierung" (On metronome markings) [Mus 139]
1929	"Musikalische Dynamik" (Musical dynamics) [SI, 341]
1930?	"Splitter" (Aphorisms on opera) [SI, 337–39]
1931	"Raumton, Vibrato, Radio, etc." (Tone space, vibrato, radio, etc.) [Mus 173a–c]
1931	"Phrasierung" (Phrasing) [SI, 347–48]
1934	"Triolen und Quartolen bei Brahms und Bach" (Triplets and quadruplets in Brahms and Bach) [Christensen and Christensen, *Literary Legacy*, "Kleine Manuscripte," III-E, 56]
1934	"Vortrag und Gestalt" (Performance and gestalt) in "Der musikalische Gedanke und die Logik, Technique und Kunst seiner Darstellung" [no. A-3c in Rufer, *Works*, 137–38]
1940?	"Das Vibrato hat man in meiner Jugend ..." (In my youth, vibrato ...) [Christensen and Christensen, *Literary Legacy*, "Dichtungen," 4i, 62, SI, 345–346]
post-1945	"Theory of Performance" [no. A-5 in Rufer, *Works*, 139]
undated	"Zur Vortragslehre" (For the manual of performance) [Mus 299a]
undated	"Theory of Performance" [Christensen and Christensen, *Literary Legacy*, "Fragmente," v-5, 44]

Table 5. *Continued*

undated	"Musical Notation is done in rebusses . . ." [Christensen and Christensen, *Literary Legacy*, "Fragmente," v-8, 45]
undated	"Today's Manner of Performing Classical Music" [SI, 320–22]

Harmony

1927/34	"Problems of harmony" [SI, 268–87]
1936–38?	"Resolution of 6-, 7-, 8-, and 9-voiced chords" [Mus 375]
1937	"Revised Version of the *Harmonielehre*" ["Unfinished Theoretical Works," no.13]
1946	*Structural Functions of Harmony*, London: Williams & Norgate, 1946; 2d ed., New York: Norton, 1948

The Twelve-Tone Method

1923	"Gesetze der Komposition mit zwölf Tönen" (Laws of composition with twelve tones) [P] [L, 104]
1924	"Gesetze der Komposition mit zwölf Tönen" (Laws of composition with twelve tones) [P] [SI, 214–49]
1925	"Zu Darstellung des Gedankens" (On the presentation of the idea) [Mus 104a/b]
1934	"Vortrag/12TK/Princeton" [Claudio Spies, "Vortrag/12TK/Princeton," *Perspectives of New Music* 13, no.1 (1974):58–136]
1941/48	"Composition with Twelve Tones" [SI, 214–49]

[a] For a discussion of the relationship of the "Theory of Composition" to "Coherence," see p.li. In 1923 Schoenberg proposed a book to be entitled "Composition with Twelve Tones," but in 1924 he decided that an article with that title was sufficient (see Schoenberg, *Letters*, 104; Arnold Schoenberg, *Style and Idea*, ed. Leonard Stein [New York: St. Martin's Press, 1975], 23–24). In 1923 he also proposed a performance text, and in 1929 a new text on harmony; see the manuscript catalogued as T37.4, 7–8 at the Arnold Schoenberg Institute and as 3a–b in Rufer, *Works*, 1937; Arnold Schoenberg, "Der musikalische Gedanke und seine Darstellung," section 2, paragraph 7; also see Schoenberg, *Style*, 319–20.

THE HEXACHORDAL EXAMPLES IN "KONTRAPUNKT"

The undated examples for "Kontrapunkt" are contained in a separately bound set of nineteen pages of J.E. & Co. no.28 music paper. Pages 1, 3, and 4 contain hexachordal sketches; pages 5 and 6 contain three exercises in tonal species counterpoint; pages 2 and 7–18 are blank. There is no verbal commentary.[26] The examples are written in lead pencil except for the subtitle "Zum Kontrapunkt" on page 1, which is in red ink. The cover of the bound sheets bears its own unique title: "Notenbeispiele zu Kontrapunkt, Formenlehre, Instrumentation u. Zusammenhang," but there are in fact no examples for "Formenlehre," "Instrumentation," or "Zusammenhang."

Though the designation "Zum Kontrapunkt" heads the initial page of hexachordal sketches and canons, it seems unlikely that Schoenberg would include such nontonal material with pedagogy in mind; it would certainly be the only such example in all his writings.[27] Instead, these examples may be understood to be compositional sketches interpolated into the material for "Kontrapunkt."

The first and third pages of hexachordal material reveal a similar format: the abstraction of a twelve-tone set and its inversionally combinatorial counterpart, followed by musical excerpts incorporating this material. According to Ethan Haimo's chronology of sketch types, Schoenberg's use of such I-H combinatoriality implies a date of composition no earlier than 1925.[28] The I-H combinations of which Haimo speaks, however, were written at a time when Schoenberg was aware of their structural implications for the twelve-tone method. The initial

---

26. Schoenberg does comment on canons and independent voices in "*Ripieno* and filler-voices," in "Kontrapunkt," concluding that the second voice of a canon is indeed an independent one.

27. The 1926 counterpoint manuscript, like the proposed texts that were meant to succeed *Preliminary Exercises in Counterpoint*, deals exclusively with tonal materials: see Schoenberg, *Preliminary Exercises*, Appendix B.

28. "The regular combination of I-H-combinatorially related sets is characteristic of Schoenberg's work from 1925 onward" (Ethan Haimo, "Redating Schoenberg's Passacaglia for Orchestra," *Journal of the American Musicological Society* 40 {1987}: 486); Ethan Haimo, *Schoenberg's Serial Odyssey: The Evolution of his Twelve-Tone Method, 1914–1928* (Oxford: Clarendon Press, 1990), 8–11, 145–48.

Facsimile 1: Hexachordal sketches

sketches in the examples for "Kontrapunkt" show a progression of triads in which Schoenberg seems to be learning about constructions with I-H combinatoriality, thus suggesting a slightly earlier date.

The first page of hexachordal sketches is distinguished by networks of relationships seemingly derived from various twelve-tone sets (see facsimile 1 and its transcription, ex. 1). As a first step, Schoenberg writes out a set and its inversion at the octave, a common procedure in his twelve-tone sketches. The first elements of both pairs of inversionally related hexachords (B and F) are at the interval of an octave (see dotted lines in ex. 2). Moreover, the composer's reordering of material at the end of the first system ends with the arpeggiation of the sound of the G♯ minor triad (circled in ex. 2). Apparently dissatisfied, Schoenberg rejects this combination and its inherent ordering and begins again.

With a new row, which retains the opening trichord of the first attempt, Schoenberg now inverts at the lower fifth, producing semicombinatoriality (ex. 3). Instead of pursuing aspects of semicombinatoriality other than that at the transposition a fifth below, Schoenberg proceeds to experiment with this second combination through the pro-

xliv *Introduction*

Example 1: Hexachordal sketches in "Zum Kontrapunkt"

xlv *Introduction*

Example 2: The first, rejected combination

Example 3: The second, I-H combination

cess of *Umlagerung* or "rearrangement."[29] First he rearranges the pitches of the first hexachord in the upper line to form a third, two-voice combination (see no.3 in ex.1); the second hexachord enters as a third voice. Next, Schoenberg writes a fourth combination, generated by the row's opening 015 trichord, and thus produces an aggregate composed of the all-combinatorial hexachord 014589 (ex.4). The canonic lines continue with 014 trichords, which also generate the 014589 all-combinatorial hexachord. Linearly, according to Schoenberg's stemming, the canonic lines contain representations of the semicombinatorial hexachord 012578 (ex.5).

Running out of space on page 1, Schoenberg numbers a second sheet

Example 4: The all-combinatorial hexachords generated by the 015 trichord

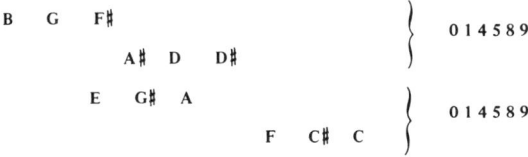

---

29. Schoenberg describes the process of *Umlagerung* in the comment "Variation," in "Der musikalische Gedanke und die Logik, Technik und Kunst seiner Darstellung," 36.

Example 5: Analysis of the canon in example 4

0 1 2 5 7 8	B A♯	G D	F♯ D♯	C A	C♯ G♯	E E♯	
0 1 2 5 7 8	E F	G♯ C♯	A C	D♯ G♯	D G	B B♭	
	0 1 4 5 8 9			0 1 4 5 8 9 :			All-Combinatorial Hexachords

Facsimile 2: Sketches for the Variations for Orchestra, op. 31, in "Zum Kontrapunkt"

to continue but ultimately leaves it blank; he never returns to this material. Nonetheless, the all-combinationarial hexachord used in this canon was to generate the set for the Suite (Septet), op. 29, composed in 1924–26, and the Passacaglia for Orchestra, begun in March 1926.[30]

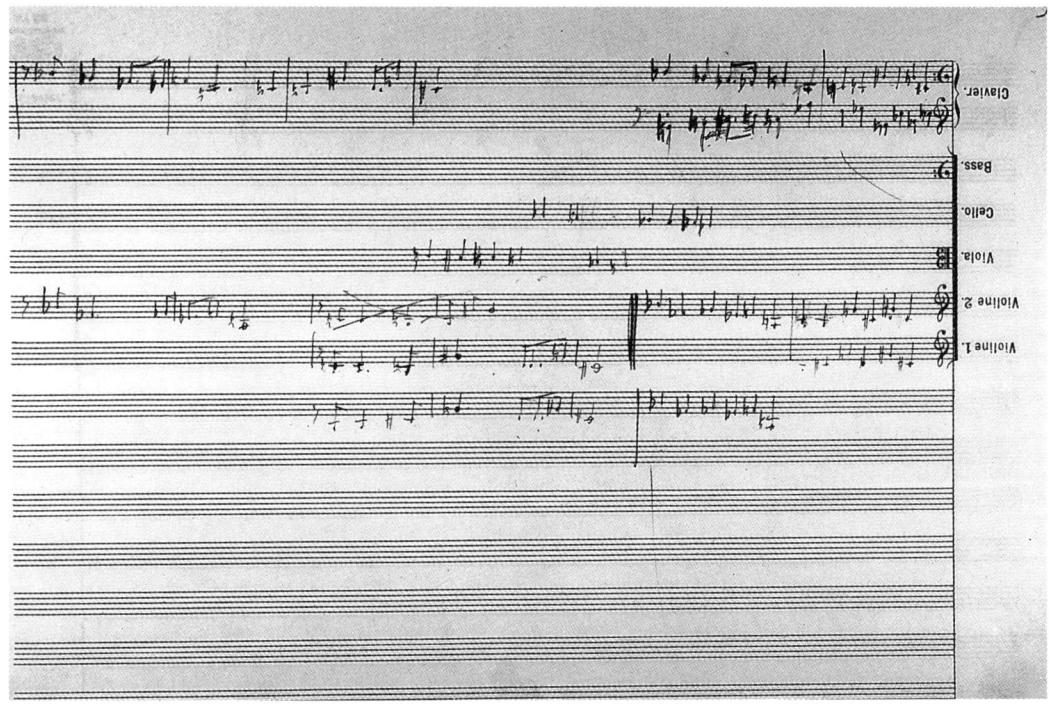

---

30. I adhere to the date proposed by Haimo, "Redating," 481. Haimo's view is documented by a discovery of Professor Reinhold Brinkmann of Harvard University: a letter from Schoenberg to Rudolf Kolisch dated March 7, 1926, in which Schoenberg mentions that he is presently working on the Passacaglia: see *Journal of the American Musicological Society* 41, no. 2 (1988): 393.

xlvii *Introduction*

As we shall see, the latter work plays an important role in relation to the other hexachordal sketches of "Zum Kontrapunkt."

The second hexachordal sheet, numbered as page 3, is of outstanding historical significance: here without doubt is a hitherto unidentified sketch for the theme of the 1926 Variations for Orchestra, op.31 (see facsimile 2 and its transcription in ex.6). Indeed, this particular sketch adds a missing link between the ultimate source of the set of the Variations for Orchestra, the sketches for the Passacaglia for Orchestra, begun on March 5, 1926, and the earliest hitherto known draft of the theme, dated May 2, 1926.[31] In fact, this sheet represents the very first draft for the theme of Opus 31.

While the Passacaglia provides the ultimate pitch content of the Variations' theme (see ex.7a), the sketch in "Zum Kontrapunkt" is the

Example 6: Sketches for the Variations for Orchestra, op.31, in "Zum Kontrapunkt"

---

31. See Rufer, *Works*, 51–52; see Haimo, "Redating," 489–91, for a detailed discussion of the preliminary set of the Variations for Orchestra.

xlviii *Introduction*

Example 7: Sources for the set of the Variations for Orchestra, op.31

a: The preliminary set in the sketch for the Passacaglia for Orchestra

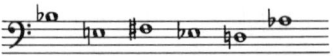

b: The draft of the theme for the Variations for Orchestra in "Zum Kontrapunkt"

c.i: The earliest hitherto known draft of the theme (May 2, 1926)

c.ii: The theme excerpted from the sketch (May 2, 1926)

d.i: The first appearance of the first hexachord in the introduction

d.i: The first appearance of the first hexachord in the introduction

d.ii: The theme in the score

source of the pitch content and order of its first hexachord. Furthermore, it is the source of the theme's surface rhythm (ex. 7b). Moreover, the partitioning of the set into divisions of five, three, and four is a characteristic of sets in the Variations as a whole. In "Zum Kontrapunkt" Schoenberg starts with a twelve-tone theme whose first seven notes could be viewed as a succession of 037 trichords. By exchanging the second and third pitches of this theme, Schoenberg produces the familiar first hexachord of the Variations for Orchestra, already close to the rhythm it will have in that work. Further studies of reorderings of the second hexachord of the theme and combinations of the original and inverted forms of the first hexachord complete the page. Note that these studies, notated in quarter notes, produce the shape the first hexachord will assume when it first appears in the introduction to Opus 31 (see ex. 7d.i below).

It seems clear that these hexachordal sketches must be dated between March 5, 1926, when Schoenberg began work on the Passacaglia for Orchestra, and May 2, 1926, when he began sketching the Variations for Orchestra (Table 6 summarizes Schoenberg's activities during this period).[32] This dating is supported by the identity of the first hexachord on page 1 of the earliest hitherto known sketch for Opus 31 and the first hexachord in the last sketch of page 3 in "Zum Kontrapunkt." Moreover, Schoenberg considers the same topic in both the earlier and later sketch: the reordering of the second hexachord (compare ex. 7b and c). The content of page 3 of "Zum Kontrapunkt" likewise shows a nine-year gap between the prose text of ZKIF and "Notenbeispiele zu Kontrapunkt, Formenlehre, Instrumentation u. Zusammenhang." Nevertheless, sometime between March 5 and May 2, 1926, Schoenberg did

---

32. Unfortunately, knowledge about J.E. & Co.'s no. 28 paper adds little information about the dating of the sheets. The paper was used at least one other time in the 1920s, for an arrangement of *Funicul'i, Funicul'a* by Luigi Denza (1921). It is interesting that early sketches for the Third String Quartet, op. 30, another work begun in March 1926, appear within the material for the song "Liebeslied," also dating from May 1917: see Reynold Simpson, "Archives Report: A Study of the U186 Sketches" (1990), unpublished report at the Arnold Schoenberg Institute, and idem, "New Sketches, Old Fragments, and Schoenberg's Third String Quartet, Op. 30," *Theory and Practice* 17 (1992).

1 Introduction

Table 6. A Summary of Dates in 1926

April 11–23, 1917; March–May, 1926: ZKIF

Begun March 5, 1926: Passacaglia for Orchestra

Begun between March 5, 1926 and May 2, 1926: "Notenbeispielen für Kontrapunkt, Formenlehre, Instrumentation u. Zusammenhang"

Begun May 2, 1926: Variations for Orchestra

Begun October 29, 1926: "Kontrapunkt" ["Unfinished Theoretical Works," no.4]

---

decide to work out contrapuntal examples for the nine-year-old ZKIF project, and in the fall of 1926, during the temporary cessation of work on the Variations for Orchestra, he did work a fair amount on the counterpoint text (see Table 4).[33] In the spring of 1926, however, his efforts in this direction were undermined. Schoenberg's intuitions led him not into the counterpoint text but into the composition of the Variations for Orchestra.

---

33. The exact date on the counterpoint text is October 29, 1926, over four months after beginning the Variations: see Rufer, *Works*, 135. Ethan Haimo points out a revealing relationship between the Variations and traditional counterpoint of Bach:

> It has been mentioned that the *Variations* constitute "a veritable 'Art of the Fugue'" of early twelve-tone technique. This remark, dropped {by Milton Babbitt} almost casually in a discussion of another work, should be taken very seriously. Not only are there obvious parallels, but also there is the explicit B-A-C-H theme that becomes the focus of the Finale. Can it be coincidental then that Schoenberg's set, at its original pitch level, contains a five-note segment that seems as if it could be used to form a theme for another Contrapunctus?
>
> Taken in isolation this resemblance might seem a bit far-fetched, but when it is seen together with the B-A-C-H motive, the appearance in the sketches of Bach-like fugal episodes in D minor, and the prominent role Bach's "Art of the Fugue" played in Schoenberg's pedagogy in the early 1920's, it should be clear that the *Variations* represented Schoenberg's homage to that composer whose music had done so much to assure the importance of German music in a previous century. (Haimo, *Odyssey*, 162–63)

Following Haimo's logic, it does not seem bizarre that the first sketch for the Variations should appear in a book on counterpoint.

THE HISTORICAL-THEORETICAL SIGNIFICANCE OF ZKIF

In his 1911 letter to Hertzka, Schoenberg wrote that he wished to view counterpoint, instrumentation, and form not as separate disciplines but as a unified whole: a concept that he planned to discuss in a work to be entitled "Aesthetic of Music." Schoenberg never mentioned the book project again in his theoretical writings. In the foreword to ZKIF, however, Schoenberg explained that he intended to present *Zusammenhang* (coherence) as a general theory[34] under which *Formenlehre* (the study of given formal structures), counterpoint (the study of the organization of melodic lines), and instrumentation could be understood.[35] It is crucial to realize that in ZKIF Schoenberg's plans for a unified theory remained unfulfilled: he never consciously related the ideas proposed in "Zusammenhang" to those presented in "Kontrapunkt," "Instrumentation," or "Formenlehre," nor did he ever truly fulfill this goal even in later manuscripts.[36] The content of "Zusammenhang" consists merely of Schoenberg's suggestive notes concerning a theory of coherence.

Table 4 includes the list of works associated with coherence. In 1922 Schoenberg planned both a "Lehre vom musikalischen Zusammenhang" [Theory of musical coherence] and a "Kompositionslehre" [Theory of composition].[37] In 1924, however, he wrote, "More recently I have made some discoveries which compelled me to revise the small work entitled *Theory of Musical Coherence* into the more ambitious *Die Gesetze der musikalischen Komposition* (The laws of musical composition)."[38] The book on coherence and the book on compositional theory

---

34. Note that Schoenberg explicitly titles the first section of Notebook I "Theory of Coherence": see pp.15, 119.

35. "Neither counterpoint nor instruction in form or instrumentation ... claim to be theories" (3). For this reason I translate *Lehre* as "theory" in relation to *Zusammenhang* but as "instruction" in relation to *Instrumentation* and *Formenlehre*.

36. The unified theory is mentioned again in Schoenberg, "Der musikalische Gedanke und seine Darstellung," section 2, paragraph 7, and in the manuscript catalogued as T37.4–6 at the Arnold Schoenberg Institute and as 3b in Rufer, *Works*, 137: Arnold Schoenberg, "Der musikalische Gedanke, seine Darstellung und Durchführung," 1 (Rufer uses a different title for this manuscript).

37. Schoenberg mentions both books in a letter to Wassily Kandinsky dated July 20, 1922: see Schoenberg, *Letters*, 71.

38. Schoenberg, *Style*, 23–24.

thus had become identified as a single project on composition. In 1925 Schoenberg began the essay "Der musikalische Gedanke, seine Darstellung und Durchführung" [The musical idea, its presentation and development], on whose cover is the title "Kompositionslehre" [Theory of composition].

The "discoveries" to which Schoenberg referred almost certainly concerned the twelve-tone method, which he began to use almost exclusively in 1923. The first manuscript entitled "Der musikalische Gedanke" (The musical idea) also dates from that year.[39] In 1923 he proposed a book to be entitled "Composition with Twelve Tones," but in 1924 decided that an article with that title was sufficient.[40] This chronology suggests that Schoenberg's work on the twelve-tone method confirmed his belief that the coherence in any piece of music (tonal or atonal, twelve-tone or not) is the expression of a single musical idea.

In the ensuing "Der musikalische Gedanke und seine Darstellung" [The musical idea and its presentation], written between 1925 and 1929, Schoenberg again brought up the idea of a unified theory of composition:

> At present the theory of harmony, counterpoint, and the theory of form mainly serve pedagogical purposes. With the possible exception of the theory of harmony, the individual disciplines completely lack even a truly theoretical basis emanating from other external criteria. On the whole, the consequence is that three different disciplines, which together should constitute the theory of composition, in reality fall apart because they lack a common point of view.[41]

By 1929 Schoenberg saw his concept of musical idea as the basis for such a unified theory of composition: "Composition . . . is above all the art of inventing a musical idea and the fitting way to present it."[42] The concept of the musical idea thus superseded the earlier general theory of coherence as the core of Schoenberg's theory of composition. In this light ZKIF can be seen as Schoenberg's first step toward formulating a unified theory of composition.

---

39. See the manuscript catalogued as T34.29 at the Arnold Schoenberg Institute.

40. Schoenberg, *Letters*, 104; idem, *Style*, 23–24.

41. Schoenberg, "Der musikalische Gedanke, seine Darstellung und Durchführung," 3 (translation by Charlotte M. Cross).

42. Schoenberg, *Style*, 374.

The sketchy, incomplete enunciation of Schoenberg's theory of coherence in "Zusammenhang" can be fleshed out from ideas propounded in the *Harmonielehre* and later works, and particularly by looking closely at Schoenberg's notion of a musical theory and his ideas of musical form. Even with its deficiencies, "Zusammenhang" is uniquely rich among Schoenberg's theoretical works in its many speculative comments on musical perception, which I shall consider here in detail. In this work also he discusses the principle of developing variation for the first time, illustrating that principle with an analysis of Mozart's "Dissonant" Quartet, K.465.

Schoenberg's Concept of Music Theory

Schoenberg's musical theories are predicated on his theory of art, which he clarifies by a comparison with a scientific hypothesis. A scientific theory must present each individual case in light of a general law that encompasses all relevant cases, Schoenberg writes, whereas a theory of art confines itself to dealing with the attributes of individual works. In art the construct is not mechanical, like a clock, for example, whose parts are set in motion according to the laws of physics. The artwork is instead an image that possesses the vital unity of a living creature: "the work of art, like every living thing, is conceived as a whole—just like a child, whose arm or leg is not conceived separately."[43] Schoenberg's musical theories rest on this notion of an organic musical artwork.

The venerable tradition of organicism has attributed three qualities to the artwork: the whole is more than the sum of its parts; a quality of wholeness is present in every detail of the work; and an alteration in the part is an alteration in the whole.[44] Schoenberg agrees with two of these attributes. He believes that a quality of wholeness pervades every detail of the artwork. For example, in his essay "The Relationship to the Text" Schoenberg speaks of his guilty realization that he did not know the texts of certain Schubert songs he so loved. Upon immediately reading

---

43. Ibid., 458. See also "Principles of Construction" in "Der musikalische Gedanke und die Logik, Technik und Kunst seiner Darstellung," 217, passim.

44. See Ruth Solie, "The Living Work: Organicism and Analysis," *Nineteenth-Century Music* 4, no.1 (1980): 7. For a more detailed discussion of Schoenberg's organicism, see Severine Neff, "Goethe and Schoenberg: Organicism and Analysis," in *Music Theory and the Exploration of the Past*, ed. Christopher Hatch and David Bernstein (Chicago: University of Chicago Press, 1993), 409–33; Patricia Carpenter, "*Grundgestalt* as Tonal Function," *Music Theory Spectrum* 5 (1983): 15–38.

them all, he found, surprisingly, that without knowing the texts he had grasped the content:

> Thence it become clear to me that the work of art is like every other complete organism. It is so homogeneous that in every little detail it reveals its truest, inmost essence. When one cuts into any part of the human body, the same thing always comes out—blood. When one hears a verse of a poem, a measure of a composition, one is in a position to comprehend the whole. Even so, a word, a glance, a gesture, the gait, even the color of the hair are sufficient to reveal the personality of the human being. So I had completely understood the Schubert songs, together with their poems from the music alone, . . . with a perfection that analysis and synthesis could hardly have attained but not surpassed.[45]

A second principle of organicism with which Schoenberg agrees is that the whole of the artwork is more than the sum of its parts. Schoenberg elucidates this principle in a comparison of parts and wholes in the mechanism and in the organism. The mechanical part works on a principle of cause and effect. For example, winding up a clock that is working properly will always cause the spring to set the separate parts in motion. The chain reaction of the parts is causal in effect, the ultimate effect being a running clock. The organic part is distinct from the mechanical one. Organic parts are not in causal relationship to one another. For example, in a musical composition the main theme of a work does not cause the second theme to happen, as if in a chain reaction. Instead, each theme presents its own relationship to the whole composition. That relationship defines the theme's function:

> True members that function, even though they may be at rest, are found only in organisms; here they are activated not by energy resulting from an inner driving power, but as a result of their organic membership in a living being.[46]

Moreover, not only are the parts perceived as functioning because of their relation to the whole, but the whole is perceived as a whole because of the total effect of the parts:

---

45. Schoenberg, *Style*, 144.

46. Schoenberg, "Der musikalische Gedanke und die Logik, Technik und Kunst seiner Darstellung," 221. Page numbers cited in this paragraph and the next refer to this text.

> Above all, a piece of music is (perhaps invariably) an articulated organism whose organs, members, carry out specific functions in regard to both their own external effect and their mutual relations. (227)

A third principle of organicism, first stated by the Roman philosopher Plotinus, held that an alteration of a part of an artwork, whether by changes, addition, or removal, involves the alteration of the *entire* work in all its manifestations. Schoenberg does not adhere to this tenet. In his discussion of functioning parts, he asserts that "an organism can do without some of its members" and still function as that organism (221).

The uniqueness of Schoenberg's views rests on his belief that the essence of a work, its musical idea, is a priori: beyond time and space, perhaps even metaphysical in nature.[47] While the idea of a work is eternal, Schoenberg points out that at first only the composer knows its essence intimately. It is the composer's task to translate the musical idea into an organic form comprehensible to a listener.

> It is one thing to envision in a creative instant of inspiration, it is another thing to materialize one's vision by painstakingly connecting details until they fuse into a kind of organism. . . . it remains another thing to organize this form so that it becomes a comprehensible message "to whom it may concern."[48]

Schoenberg believes that in the process of composition a composer can present the idea in many ways without changing its essence, so long as his structural choices fuse into a whole that has the characteristics of an organism. Such an alteration of parts can profoundly affect the presentation of the whole, but not the idea itself, the essence of the organism:

> Even a small alteration in the basic structure of an organism has far-reaching consequences. . . . It is certain that if such an alteration is alien to the nature of this organism, then the majority of its consequences will be harmful, and the apparent necessity that induced the alteration is traced back to an incorrect judgment. If, however, the alteration really agrees with the nature of the organism, with its devel-

---

47. See p.5.

48. Schoenberg, *Style*, 215.

opmental tendencies, then there will result from such an objectively correct measure not only those advantages one expected but others, as well, that one had not aimed for. And, conversely, if one starts with the desire to gain new effects from the organism, effects inherent in its nature, then it will always turn out that one has at the same time been obeying a necessity of this organism, that one has been promoting its developmental tendencies.[49]

Schoenberg's study of organic presentation shaped his theoretical thought. As he points out in the *Harmonielehre*, however, his values placed him at odds with contemporary music theorists, whom he viewed as uninterested in the presentation of the idea as organism. He saw them as interested instead in determining general laws for describing musical events; they took more pleasure in their system than in the object: the living thing is replaced with the system (8). Schoenberg thus equated the work of contemporary theory with mechanistic systems that were antithetical to art:

> It is indeed our duty to reflect over and over again upon the mysterious origins of the powers of art (*Kunstwirkungen*). And again and again begin at the beginning; again and again to examine anew for ourselves and attempt to organize anew for ourselves, regarding nothing as given but the phenomena. These we may more rightly regard as eternal than the laws we believe we have found. Since we do definitely know (*wissen*) the phenomena [as facts] we might be more justified in giving the name, "science" (*Wissenschaft*) to our [direct] knowledge (*Wissen*) of the phenomena, rather than those conjectures that are intended to explain them.
>
> Yet these conjectures, too, have their justification: as experiments . . . perhaps sometimes even as preliminary steps to truth. . . .
>
> If art theory could be content with that, . . . one could not object to it. But it is more ambitious. . . . it professes to have found *the eternal* laws. . . . But now begins the error. For it is falsely concluded that these laws, since apparently correct with regard to the phenomena previously observed, must then hold true for all future phenomena as well. (8)

---

49. Arnold Schoenberg, *Theory of Harmony*, trans. Roy E. Carter (Berkeley and Los Angeles: University of California Press, 1978), 53. Page numbers cited in the text for the remainder of this section refer to this work.

Schoenberg further argued against general theoretical laws by virtue of his definition of music as dependent on three factors:

> The material of music is the tone; what it affects first, the ear. The sensory perception releases associations and connects tone, ear, and the world of feeling. On the cooperation of these three factors depends everything in music that is felt to be art. (19)

The theoretical investigation of these factors, however, provokes a myriad of problems if one looks for general laws. On one hand, Schoenberg points out that "the world of feelings . . . completely eludes precisely controlled investigation." On the other hand, the study of the tone in a musical sense must relate to the variable "constitution of the ear, the organ predetermined to receive tone" (19). Finally, Schoenberg believed that any general premises about music were impossible without a cogent theory of perception: "unsurmountable difficulties lie in the way of analysis if the impression on the observing subject is now taken as the point of departure for inquiry" (18). Without a theory of perception or of the physiology of hearing, he concludes, no theory can be "correct" in the sense of an axiom of science. Instead, as theorists "we can only base our thought on such conjectures as will satisfy our formal necessity for sense and coherence without their being considered natural laws" (19).

Schoenberg's theoretical work, including "Zusammenhang," is based on his intuitions about the presentation of organic form: "whenever I theorize, it is less important whether these theories be right than whether they be useful as comparisons to clarify the object and to give the study perspective. . . . [Theory] should affirm, describe, compare, and organize (19, 345). These intuitions are above all those of a composer who is constantly "drawing consequences" from the material he is studying, whether his own composition or that of someone else. As Schoenberg said, "I am more a composer . . . than theorist."[50]

Musical Form and the Theory of Coherence

Schoenberg lays out a sequence of ideas for "Zusammenhang" beginning with an introduction that points to the purpose of the book:

> *Introduction:* The theory of composition . . . provides empirically based instructions for achieving musical results.

---

50. Schoenberg, *Style*, 213.

> Here the justification for employing such means should be examined. This investigation presupposes the assertion that:
>
> > tones, harmonies, rhythms are the parts that, if correctly joined, make up the musical result.
>
> And now the question arises:
>
> > *Which are the connections between tones, harmonies, and rhythms insofar as these are intended to constitute a musical form?*
>
> The formulation of such connections will lead to the recognition of *structural* principles.[51]

The main issue of "Zusammenhang," as of many subsequent theoretical works, is the "how" of presenting a musical form, for Schoenberg always an organic form:

> The form of a composition is achieved because 1) a body exists, and because 2) the members exercise different functions and are created for these functions.[52]

The goal of such a form is comprehensibility: the logical organization of the composer's idea so that it is grasped by a listener:

> To organize something means to build it so that its parts function, that is, work together for a common purpose. Accordingly, a piece consists of parts, limbs, organs like every other living creature; and whatever might be the tendency of the actual musical contents, their principle function will be to produce an intelligent and intelligible impression on a listener.[53]

Despite his previous recognition of the difficulties of such a theory, in "Zusammenhang" Schoenberg makes an attempt—albeit a sketchy one—to approach the understanding of musical form as a problem of perception itself.

Understanding, Comprehensibility, and Form

In the *Harmonielehre*, Schoenberg points out:

> As Schopenhauer shows in his theory of colors . . . a real theory should start with the subject. . . . one would have to go back to the subject, to the sense of hearing, if one were to establish a real theory

---

51. See p.7.

52. Schoenberg, *Style*, 257.

53. Schoenberg, "Form" (catalogued as D-180 in Rufer, *Works*, 162), 1.

of tones. Now it is not my aim to present such a theory . . . nor do I possess enough ability and knowledge to do so.[54]

Despite his disclaimer, Schoenberg does subsequently speculate about the act of listening and the understanding of a work. For instance, in his text for the unfinished 1914 Symphony, he describes the experienced listener's perception:

> So many and each single thing seems important. . . . Now it sings; each sings something different thinking that it sings the same thing; and in fact, sounds in one dimension together, . . . in another diverse. In a third and fourth it sounds still otherwise which one cannot express. It has countless dimensions and each one is perceivable. And all disappear to some place where they could be found. It would be easy to pursue them, for now one has their intuitive contemplation [*Anschauung*].[55]

Note how at first, "each single thing seems important"; next, "each thing sings something different" but thinks it is the same; finally, the diverse elements "sound in one dimension together," as perceptions "disappear" into a whole that the mind has constructed. This process of creating the imagined work in the mind of the listener—understood instantaneously, irrespective of time—is the result of "intuitive contemplation." This is the way a listener assimilates the musical form that expresses the composer's idea.

Schoenberg uses different words to describe such understanding of a work through intuitive contemplation. *Comprehensibility* (*Fasslichkeit*) emphasizes the conditions of coherence grasped during the temporal unfolding of a piece: it is "to analyse quickly," to apprehend "in the small amount of time granted us by the flow of the events, . . . recognize . . . figures . . . the way they hang together, as well as their meaning."[56] *Understanding* (*Verstehen*) is used to describe the same process out of time, the reconsideration of the imagined work as an organic form in all its manifestations.[57] Comprehensibility of the work rests

---

54. Schoenberg, *Theory of Harmony*, 18.

55. Quoted in Walter B. Bailey, *Programmatic Elements in the Works of Schoenberg* (Ann Arbor, Mich.: UMI, 1984), 98–99.

56. Schoenberg, *Theory of Harmony*, 133; idem, "Opinion or Insight," *Style*, 259.

57. "Understanding is based on memory" (Schoenberg, "Der musikalische Gedanke und die Logik, Technik und Kunst seiner Darstellung," 7).

on direct experience, understanding on memory: recognition and re-recognition. Comprehensibility thus focuses on the moment itself; understanding allows time to recognize parts and compare relationships between them.

In "Zusammenhang," Schoenberg uses an analogy to describe the process of recognition that he called understanding:

> A wardrobe is to be opened, but the unknown key to it is not at hand. Before resorting to the locksmith, one gathers up all the keys in the house, since all locks require a key. A number of keys that are definitely much too large or much too small are immediately excluded, without even trying them out. The first that seems possible is too large, the next too small: yet all was not in vain, because one now has an approximate idea of the size. The next has a completely wrong shape. One tries a differently shaped fourth key. Finally after [trying] many [keys], one is found that, although it can be completely turned in the lock, still does not work. Now, however, one knows the lock somewhat, and has rejected so many keys that only a small number are left. Despite this effort it is usually necessary to wait for the locksmith, but now and then the right key can be found in this way, or one may learn how a similar key must be filed so it might lock.[58]

The comparison of keys to the lock rests on learned knowledge of keys and locks and on a clear understanding of the whole situation. The purpose is to find the key, and each act is a function of it. The actual understanding, Schoenberg says, rests on "the capacity to recognize the similarity" (15) between one key and another:

> The presupposition for this *recognition of similarity* is the capacity of memory: to remember new and old components. . . . *To understand a thing, it is necessary to recognize that in many (or, if possible, in all) of its parts, it may be similar or even identical to things or parts that are familiar.* (11)

Thus one recognizes a thing for what it is.

Familiarity sets up a comparison between the recognized and the un-

---

58. See p. 13; all subsequent page numbers cited in the text refer to the present edition of ZKIF.

known. For Schoenberg, to theorize is to compare. The comparative study of musical events rests on two principles: coherence and comprehensibility.

> However much I may theorize, I do so with constant and full awareness that I am only presenting comparisons, in the sense indicated above; symbols, which are merely intended to connect ideas apparently remote from one another, to promote intelligibility through coherence of presentation, and to show the wealth of ways in which all facts relate to an idea.[59]

Schoenberg defines artistic coherence as that which connects one musical event to another with the aim of producing an art form:

> it is certainly impossible to speak of an artistic coherence if, for example, parts are connected as in the following case:
>   A strip of paper is glued to a piece of cork; a chicken feather is glued to this, to which a nail is tied with string. (61)

The principle on which such artistic coherence rests is repetition: "two ideas cohere if one of them contains a part of the other" (17). The nature and degree of repetition from event to event, however, can produce very different structural principles: "simple, logical coherence" (3), contrast, or change and variation:

> *Coherence* comes into being when parts that are partly the same, partly different, are connected so that those parts that are the same become prominent.
>   *Contrast* (relational) is likewise based on coherence, insofar as the same parts as mentioned above are connected so that the unlike parts predominantly attract attention.
>   *Change and variation* are based on repetition, insofar as several of the like parts as well as several of the dissimilar parts become discernible. Development is one such succession of related ideas, in which unlike parts, initially subordinate in importance, gradually become the main idea. (21–23)

Through these differing ways of producing artistic coherence, the musical form takes shape.

---

59. Schoenberg, *Theory of Harmony*, 11–12.

The aim of coherence can be nothing other than comprehensibility:

> Something is *comprehensible* if the *whole . . . consists of parts* that have relationships not too remote from each other and from the whole . . . and if the arrangement of these parts is such that their relationship to each other and to the whole is not lost. (23)

Comprehensibility results from particular conditions of coherence: the binding together of components in such a way that the functioning parts are not too long or short in duration: "surveyable," "neither too large nor too small for our sense perception" (23). The presence of coherence, however, does not always guarantee comprehensibility. Comprehensibility first depends on the nature and degree of repetition of parts. Particularly in a temporal art such as music, Schoenberg says that repetition allows an idea to be grasped more readily (105). Furthermore, the nature of the repetition can effect the degree of comprehensibility. For example, the more a part is strictly repeated in terms of pitch, duration, color, or dynamic, the more recognizable it is: in Schoenberg's terms, the "stronger" its comprehensibility (17). A composer can work differently with the "essential" components of a composition, presenting them in a fairly literal or "conspicuous" way or in a more varied, "inconspicuous" fashion (19). Through these means he shapes the parts of a musical form.

Comprehensibility, however, depends not only on a composer's skill in presenting material logically and coherently, but also on the receptivity and skill of the listener, who perceives the logic and nature of coherence:

> The limits of comprehensibility are not the limits of coherence, which can be present even when comprehensibility has ceased. For there are connections inaccessible to consciousness. Such connections possibly have an effect on more experienced and trained [individuals]. (9)

Moreover, comprehensibility "can be reduced to a minimum if the performer is little concerned with his listeners' capacities of comprehension" (19). Comprehensibility thus rests on three factors: (1) the composer's skill in presenting the idea, (2) the performer's skill in interpreting it, and (3) most crucially, the listener's ability to grasp [*fassen*] and ultimately understand [*verstehen*] the idea in the act of listening.

Motive and Developing Variation

Schoenberg believes that a work's potential for comprehensibility and understanding depends on the coherence of its smallest components:

> A musical content is *musically comprehensible* if its smallest and small components (*periods, sentences, phrases, motives*) share such coherence among each other and with the whole as would in general be required for comprehensibility. (25)

Most crucial, however, is the motive itself, without which the logic of a work could be neither coherent nor comprehensible:

> Since the *motive* turns out to be the smallest part (smallest common denominator) of a piece of music, in general the presence of this smallest part in every larger part may guarantee that comprehensibility will be achieved. (25)

In his extant writings, Schoenberg gives several definitions for the term *motive*. In "Zusammenhang" he writes:

> A motive is a sounding, rhythmicized phenomenon that, by its (possibly varied) repetitions in the course of a piece of music, is capable of creating the impression that it is the material of the piece. (29)

This definition is so broad that for Schoenberg a motive can even be a single pitch of a given duration or an interval with a characteristic rhythm: "a unit which contains one or more features of interval and rhythm whose presence is manifested in constant use throughout a piece."[60]

Schoenberg states in "Zusammenhang" that the motive is the source of logical progression within a musical form: "something that gives rise to a motion" (27). This motion can be comprehended as the result of four "structuring principles" that vary the motive: repetition, contrast, change, and development (37). In the musical form, such variations of motives can either have local significance or be crucial in "allowing new ideas to arise" (39). This second method of motivic variation Schoenberg calls *developing variation*: "varied" in the sense of the motive itself, "developing" in the sense of creating a progression of logical and comprehensible connections. Developing variation has a profound effect on

---

60. Schoenberg, *Models for Beginners in Composition* (New York: G. Schirmer, 1942), 15.

articulating larger segments of a musical form: for example, the introduction of "new" motives can characterize and hence differentiate the main and subordinate functions of phrases or even sections of a piece. The illustration of developing variation in "Zusammenhang" is not only the first discussion of this principle in Schoenberg's theoretical works but also Schoenberg's first major analysis recorded in prose.[61] Significantly, he chose the first movement of Mozart's "Dissonant" Quartet, K.465, which he regarded as a precursor of his own compositions in its treatment of tonality and dissonance (see facsimile 3).[62] As mentioned above, this analysis, referred to seventeen years later in "Der musikalische Gedanke und die Logik, Technik und Kunst seiner Darstellung," is the most detailed explication of developing variation in Schoenberg's writings.[63]

In "Zusammenhang" Schoenberg states that the employment of developing variation must "proceed more or less directly toward the goal of allowing new ideas to arise" (39). For this reason the principle of developing variation is particularly crucial at a developmental point of a work: for example, the transition from the first to second group of the exposition in a sonata-allegro form, exactly the part of K.465 that Schoenberg analyzes. He wishes to show how the "new" motivic material of the first figure of the second group (m.57)[64] is derived from the material of the transition (see ex.8). He describes this passage as "one of the most perfect examples of developing variation" (43).

In developing variation the specific developments of interval and rhythm are dictated by the nature of the formal functioning part, in this

---

61. Brief analytic comments exist in the *Harmonielehre*: see, for example, remarks on Brahms's Third Symphony in Schoenberg, *Theory of Harmony*, 164.

62. "Modern music has centered interest on two problems: that of tonality, and that of dissonance. It cannot be said that the conflict regarding these questions is new, nor that it is waged with weapons. On the contrary: just as all the battlefields of world history are constantly the scene of renewed strife, so, too, is this one; this also is a battlefield in the historic sense. Of course, it is not necessary for me to cite as proof the well-known precedents from the musical past. It is enough to recall the '*Dissonance*' Quartet of Mozart" (Schoenberg, *Style*, 268).

63. See Schoenberg, "Der musikalische Gedanke und die Logik, Technik und Kunst seiner Darstellung," 34a. See also Walter Frisch, *Brahms and the Principle of Developing Variation* (Berkeley and Los Angeles: University of California Press, 1984).

64. Schoenberg termed the "second group" the "contrast."

Facsimile 3: Page 12 of ZKIF, Notebook I: the discussion of developing variation

Example 8: Schoenberg's analysis of K.465, first movement

case a transition. Later, in *Fundamentals of Musical Composition*, Schoenberg describes the characteristics of a transition:

> The purpose of a transition is not only to introduce a contrast; it is itself a contrast. It may begin, after the end of the main theme, with new thematic formulations. . . . The structure of a transition ordinarily includes four elements: establishment of the transitional idea (through repetition, often sequential); modulation (often in several stages); liquidation of motival characteristics; and establishment of a suitable upbeat chord. These aspects may overlap in varying degree.[65]

The transition in the Mozart quartet consists of three segments: measures 44–49, the variation of the main theme and the move to the dominant; measures 49–53, the development of the "new" transitional theme and the move to the V/V; and measures 53–57, the final progression to the dominant and the introduction of the first figure of the second group.

In the first segment of the transition, the basic motive of the main theme, a fifth with an upbeat rhythm is reduced to an augmented fourth with a downbeat rhythm (see ex.9). This form of the theme in the cello "prepares for" its varied presentation in the second violin. The interplay of pitch and rhythm here is typical of developing variation: the pitches remain the same, but the rhythm changes between the cello and violin

---

65. Schoenberg, *Fundamentals*, 178–79.

Example 9: The main theme and the cello preparation for the second violin

part. Schoenberg sees this new rhythm as crucial because it introduces the sixteenth-note value, which will pervade the first figure of the second group. In pitch content this second violin line is a retrograde or inversion of the same figure (ex.10).

Example 10: The second violin and the figure at m.57

The second segment of the transition introduces a "new" motive, *a*, by means of an extension of the final interval of the principal motive of the main theme: the major second becomes a minor third, which then forms part of a descending triad. The rhythm of motive *a* in measure 49 and of its variant motive *a1* in measure 50 restores the downbeat metric positioning of the cello's descent at measure 47 as well as the sixteenth-note value of the second violin at measure 48. Perhaps because the structural parallels between measures 48 and 57 occur only in the violins, Schoenberg sees the use of the same instrumentation for the imitation in measure 50 as "acquiring [structural] significance." Motive *a1* in measure 50 is further varied in pitch at measure 51 to create motive *a2*.

The third segment of the transition is introduced by the simultaneous use of the ascending third derived from motive *a1* against motive *a2* in the second violin and viola. The ascending contour is significant here because it prefigures that of the first violin at measure 57 in the second group. Schoenberg notes that subsequent variations of motive *a* further aid the listener's memory in comprehending the events of the excerpt. For example, it is possible to see the rising tritone, *a3*, as recalling the second violin at measure 48 (ex.11). Schoenberg notes in particular

Example 11: Motive *a3* and the second violin at m.48

Example 12: Relationships of motives *a1* and *a4* and the figure at m.57

the analogy between *a4* and *a1*, the repeated minor third in sixteenth notes. The third in *a4* is F♯–A, the first third of the figure in measure 57 (ex.12).

Schoenberg's method of developing variation lies at the center of his theory of coherence because it ideally suits his belief in the artwork as an organic form. The features of the motive can mutate to create an ever-changing progression of material that is still connected to earlier motives through the interplay of rhythm and pitch. Moreover, the progression can work itself out in such a way that it articulates, by means of pitch, duration, attack pattern, dynamic, or instrumentation, a functioning part of the form, which thus becomes surveyable and memorable: in sum, comprehensible to a listener. The recognition of such wholes and parts within a work allows a listener to understand the work and the composer's presentation of the musical idea. In these senses developing variation is the epitome of Schoenberg's theory of artistic coherence as discussed in "Zusammenhang": comprehensible musical forms resulting from the binding together of motives and figures.

CONCLUSION

Though it is an incomplete work containing many unfinished thoughts in outline form — mere jottings to himself — ZKIF is a crucial document for understanding Schoenberg's theoretical thought. It touches upon the major concerns of Schoenberg's musical and intellectual life — comprehensibility, coherence, organic form, motive, and orchestral and contrapuntal technique — and thus can be viewed as a basic source of his theoretical work. ZKIF is the historical source of his idea of a unified theory of composition; it is his sole work that focuses on perceptual issues such as understanding and comprehensibility. In addition, it is one of the few theoretical treatises that discusses his analytic concept of developing variation. Finally, perhaps by chance, perhaps knowingly, Schoenberg placed the first sketch of the Variations for Orchestra, a major twelve-tone work, in the examples for "Kontrapunkt." Thus the jottings of ZKIF must be read not only as skeletal fragments of musical thought fleshed out through later writings, but also as a crucial musical-intellectual self-portrait: Schoenberg's suggestive notes distilled by his attempt to jot down his "entire activities as a writer on music."

Note on the Texts

Schoenberg's *Coherence, Counterpoint, Instrumentation, Instruction in Form* is presented here in both the original German and English translation.[66] I have added headings in braces to define topical sections. Within each section of the manuscript, Schoenberg's spacing, symbols, paragraphing, punctuation, and marginalia are preserved as much as possible. Especially because of the fragmentary and incomplete nature of the manuscript, editorial additions — even punctuation and spelling — have been clearly indicated in braces in the hope of ensuring clarity, while at the same time preserving the integrity of the original work. The translation itself is as close as possible to Schoenberg's prose, virtually word for word.

The text contains three types of explanatory notes. Schoenberg's own footnotes appear within the body of the manuscript. The notes on the German text comment on matters of transcription or translation and offer corrections of the most problematic grammatical errors. Arabic footnotes in the English text are exclusively editorial remarks, including interpretations of text and symbols, identification of musical examples, and references to similar theoretical concerns in Schoenberg's other published and unpublished works.

The text contains several idiosyncracies characteristic of Schoenberg's unpublished manuscripts:

1. The symbols —— o —— and —— x —— designate the ends of sections of texts.

2. Arrows either rearrange material on pages or point out related issues between specific words.

---

66. The German transcription is based on that of Anita Luginbühl at the Arnold Schoenberg Institute.

3. Significant words are often doubly or even triply underlined for emphasis. Schoenberg's underlines are reproduced here as italics, his double underlines as italics with underline.

4. Boxed words or scale step numbers single out issues for further comment or call attention to crucial definitions of terms; boxed numerals refer to given pages of text or are dates of composition.

5. The symbol % designates a continuation of text.

6. Large exclamation marks in margins call attention to specific sentences within paragraphs.

7. Circled words designate terms needing future discussion.

I have included the editorial symbol * * * to separate material inserted on loose pages from the main body of text.

Coherence, Counterpoint, Instrumentation, Instruction in Form

ZUSAMMENHANG

KONTRAPUNKT

INSTRUMENTATION

FORMENLEHRE

{Foreword}

{II:9} 20/4.1917
in einem
Vorwort könnte gesagt werden (gut ausgeführt!):
   Weder Kontrapunkt, noch Formenlehre, noch Instrumentationslehre beanspruchen (im Gegensatz zur Harmonielehre) als Theorien zu gelten. Daher drängt sich hier der Gedanke auf:
   (fast) *alle Beispiele den Werken der Meister zu entnehmen.*
   Das könnte (so weit es ohne Zwang geht{)}, in den 4 Büchern überall durchgeführt werden.

—— o ——

{Zusammenhang}

{1:35} {BOOK OUTLINES}

Versuch einer Disposition zum *Zusammenhang*

       1. Theil
⎧ I Der einfach logische Zushg.
⎨ II Die Inversion des einf. log. Zshgs.
⎩ III Die Stilprinzipien des log. Zshgs.

{Foreword}

{II:9}[1]

20/4.1917
in a
foreword it could be stated (well executed!):

Neither counterpoint nor instruction in form or instrumentation (in contrast to the theory of harmony) claim to be theories. For this reason the thought insistently comes up

of taking (almost) *all examples from the works of masters.*

This could be implemented everywhere in the 4 books (provided it can be done without forcing the issue).[2]

— o —

{Coherence}

{I:35}

{BOOK OUTLINES}

An attempt at a sequence of ideas for *coherence*

1st Part

- I Simple, logical coherence
- II The inverse of simple, logical coherence
- III The stylistic principles of logical coherence

---

1. The roman number indicates the source notebook of the excerpt; the arabic, Schoenberg's page number.

2. For further inquiry into the relation of disciplines, see Schoenberg, "Der musikalische Gedanke und seine Darstellung," section 2, paragraph 7; idem, "Der musikalische Gedanke, seiner Darstellung und Durchführung," 1.

4 *Zusammenhang*

 IV Der metaphysische Zshg.
 V Verhältnis des metaphysischen Zshgs. zum log. {Zusammenhang} (Korrespondenz)
 VI Der psychologische Zshg.
 VII Korrespondenz des psycholog. Zshgs. mit dem log. u. metaph.

II. Theil

 I Die Idee[1] eines Tonstückes ist

	1) in der Konzeption	a) rein materiell
		c) psychologisch
		b) metaphysisch
	2) in der Darstellung	a) logisch
		c) psychologisch
		b) metaphysisch

* * *

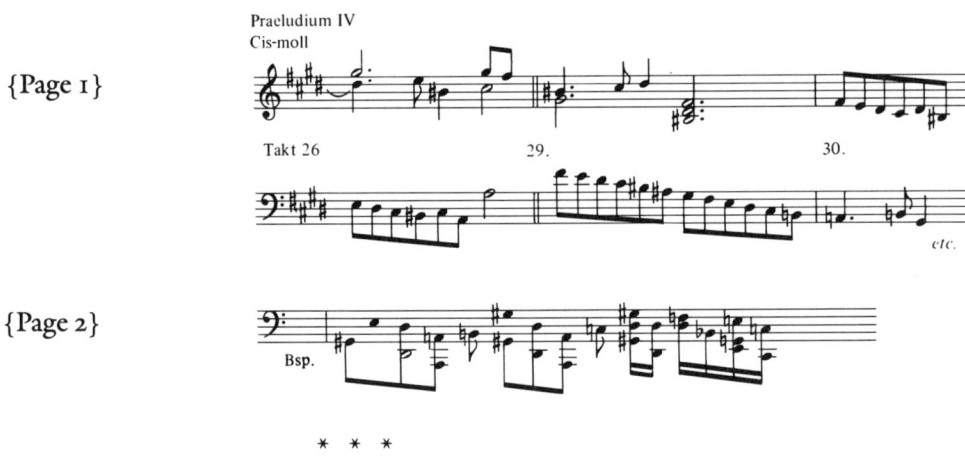

{Page 1}

{Page 2}

* * *

{1:36} II Die Konzeption hat Logik nicht nötig
   III Die Darstellung hat Logik nötig

---

1. Schoenberg's use of the word *Idee* can be equivalent to his use of *Gedanke*. In "Der musikalische Gedanke, seine Darstellung und Durchführung," he uses the terms in apposition: see p.4 of that manuscript. For a discussion of uses of "idea," see Schoenberg, *The Musical Idea and the Logic, Technique, and Art of Its Presentation*, iii.

5 *Coherence*

    IV   Metaphysical coherence
    V   Relation of metaphysical to logical coherence (correspondence)
    VI   Psychological coherence
    VII   Correspondence of psychological to logical and metaphysical coherence

2d Part

I.   the idea of a piece of music is
    1) in its conception   a) purely material
                                  c) psychological
                                  b) metaphysical
    2) in its presentation   a) logical
                                  c) psychological
                                  b) metaphysical

* * *

{Page 1}³

{Page 2}

* * *

{1:36}   II   The conception does not require logic
            III   The presentation requires logic

---

3. At this point in the text, between pp. 35 and 36, Schoenberg inserts two small sheets, whose contents are presented here as "Page 1" and "Page 2." The first sheet contains a comment on the C♯ Minor Prelude of Bach's *Well-Tempered Clavier*, Book 1; the other is an original sketch illustrating the diminution of initial material. Their specific relation to the main manuscript is unclear.

        a) wenn sie breite Verständlichkeit anstrebt
        b) solange der Autor selbst zur Intention nicht das nötige Vertrauen hat
        c) als sichtbares (äusseres) Symptom einer inneren Logik
IV Die Darstellung kann auf Logik verzichten,
        a) wenn keine breite Verständlichkeit angestrebt wird
        b) wenn der Autor der Intuition vertraut;
        c) weil das Vorhandensein äusserer logischer Symptome nicht {auf} die innere, und innere nicht auf äussere angewiesen ist.

III Theil
Verhältnis des Zshgs. zum Schönheits-Begriff

IV. Theil
Die musikalische Technik und die verschiedenen Arten des Zshgs.

—— o ——

{II:21}   21/4.1917   Entwurf zur Disposition der *Lehre vom Zusammenhang*

Einleitung: Kompositionslehre (alle 4 Disciplinen) geben empirisch gefundene Anweisungen zur Erzielung musikalischer Wirkungen.

Hier soll untersucht werden worauf sich die Berechtigung zur Anwendung solcher Mittel stützt. Diese Untersuchung geht von der Behauptung aus:

Töne, Harmonien, Rhyt{h}men sind die Teile, die auf rechte Art zusammengefügt{,} die musikalische Wirkung ausmachen.

Und {nun} stellt {sich} die Frage:

Welches sind die Zusammenhänge zwischen Tönen{,} Harmonien und Rhyt{h}men sofern diese eine musikalische Form bilden sollen{?}

Die Aufstellung der Zusammenhänge wird zur Erkenntnis der *formbildenden Principien* führen.

(Abschweifung: diese Art der Betrachtung ist gewiss sowenig die einzig zufällige wie es die bisherigen waren. Aber sie verspricht Einheitlichkeit und neue Ausblicke, da das gefundene Prinzip vielfach anwendbar ist)

a) if it aims at general intelligibility
b) so long as the author does not himself have the necessary trust in his intention
c) as a perceptible (external) symptom of an internal logic

IV The presentation can dispense with logic
a) if no general intelligibility is aimed at
b) if the author trusts his intuition
c) because the presence of external symptoms does not depend on internal logic, and internal logic does not depend on the external.[4]

3d Part

Relationship of coherence to the concept of beauty

4th Part

Musical technique and the various kinds of coherence

— o —

21/4.1917 Sketch for Assembling a Sequence of the *Theory of Coherence*

Introduction: The theory of composition (all 4 disciplines) provides empirically based instructions for achieving musical results.
Here the justification for employing such means should be examined. This investigation presupposes the assertion that:
    tones, harmonies, rhythms are the parts that, if correctly joined, make up the musical result.
    And now the question arises:
Which are the connections between tones, harmonies, and rhythms insofar as these are intended to constitute a musical form?
    The formulation of such connections will lead to recognition of *structural principles*.
    (Digression: this type of reflection is surely no more singularly coincidental than other approaches to date. Yet it promises unity and new points of view, since the discovered principle is applied in various ways)

---

4. For definitions of and statements about musical logic, see Schoenberg, *Fundamentals*, 16; idem, *Letters*, 106; idem, *Style*, 87, 104, 244; idem, unpublished manuscript "Merkmale der Logik" (Characteristics of logic), Mus 269, at the Arnold Schoenberg Institute.

I. Teil

I. *Begriff* des Zshgs Siehe 1/20–2.3 Zshg beruht auf Wiederholung
Siehe. I 22   1/1. 1/4–5. |1/10!!!| |1/22!!!|

II. Der Zshg ist das, was die Einzelerscheinungen zu *Formen* verbindet

III. Eine Form (Erscheinungsform) ist *Kunstform, wenn die* als solche erkennbaren *Zusammenhänge*, wenige deren ihre einzelnen Bestandteile miteinander verbunden sind, in gleicher Weise *für den Bestandteil, wie für das Ganze wesentlich sind*

IV. Die künstlerische[^(?)] Ausnützung des *Zshgs* zielt auf *Fasslichkeit* ab.
Siehe 1/20.4.5.6   1/4f

V. *Fasslichkeit* ist eine *Forderung*
  a) der *Mitteilungsbedürftigen*
  b) der *Aufnahmenslustigen*.

{II:22}

7. *Je fasslicher* eine Form und ein Inhalt, desto *breiter* ist der *Kreis* derjenigen auf die *er wirkt*.[^2]

Je schwerfasslicher, desto *kleiner*

8. *Der Grad der Fasslichkeit* hängt von der Art und Zahl der benützten Zshge ab (siehe auch Heft 1/20)

9. Die Grenzen des Fasslichen sind nicht die Grenzen des Zusammenhangs. Der kann auch da sein, wo Fasslichkeit aufgehört hat. Denn es giebt Zshge, die hinter dem Bewusstsein liegen. Solche wirken dann eventuell auf besser Vor- oder Ausgebildete.

II. Teil

I. Der musikalische Zshg. basiert auf den Eigenschaften des Materials und den physischen und psychischen {Eigenschaften} des Aufnehmenden.

II. Das Material des Tones bietet

---

2. sie wirken.

9 Coherence

1st Part

I. *Concept* of coherence: see 1/20–23,[5] Coherence is based on repetition: see I 22   1/1, 1/4–5. |1/10!!!| |1/22!!!|

II. Coherence is what binds individual phenomena into *forms*.

III. A form (form in appearance) is an <u>*art form if the*</u> recognizable *connections*, a few of whose individual components are connected, *are essential* in the same way *for the part as for the whole*.

IV. The artistic^(?) exploitation of *coherence* aims at *comprehensibility*. See 1/20.4.5.6   1/4f[6]

V. *Comprehensibility* is a *requirement*
   a) of *those in need of communication*
   b) of *those whose perceptions are keen*.

{II:22}

7.[7] The *more comprehensible* a form and a content, the *larger the circle* of those *affected* by it.

The more difficult to comprehend, the *smaller*

8. The *degree of comprehensibility* depends on the type and number of connections used (see also notebook 1/20)[8]

9. The limits of comprehensibility are not the limits of coherence, which can be present even where comprehensibility has ceased. For there are connections inaccessible to consciousness. Such connections possibly have an effect on more experienced or trained {individuals}.

2d Part

I. Musical coherence is based on the characteristics of the material and on the physical and psychological {characteristics} of the listener.

II. The material of the tone offers[9]

---

5. Schoenberg's citations may be found in the present volume as follows: 1/20–22: 17–19; 1/23: 21–23; 1/1: 15–17; 1/4, 5: 23–25; 1/10: 29–31; 1/22: 21–23.

6. 1/20: 17–19; 1/4: 23; 1/5: 25; 1/6 is blank; 1/4f: 23.

7. It is unclear why Schoenberg here altered his numbering system.

8. The page number is questionable because of illegibility. Schoenberg's page 1/20 corresponds to pp.17–19.

9. Schoenberg left this sentence unfinished.

10 *Zusammenhang*

{II:29}

Notizen für Zusammenhang

Mittelbar kann der Zusammenhang auch ohne inhaltliche Gemeinsamkeit {sein}, wenn der *Zweck* gemeinsam ist.

IV. Zusammenhang durch teilweise Gleichheit von Teilen
V. Die Grade des Zusammenhanges III 2 u 3

Die musikalische Verbindungstechnik

Achtung! Die Anfangs gebrauchten Beispiele weiter verwenden

Anhang: einige Analysen

Ähnlich ist: teils gleich, teils verschieden

(Klang)

{II:30}

Der *Ton* hat folgende Eigenschaften: Höhe, Dauer, Farbe und Stärke
er kann: höher und tiefer werden, kurz und lang dauern, verschiedene Farben und Stärkegrade haben.

Der *Rhyt{h}mus*

Die *Dauer* {ist} eine Eigenschaft des *Klanges und Tones* in der Musik

{ON COHERENCE AND COMPREHENSIBILITY}

{II:35}

Verstehen = Erkennen der Ähnlichkeit

§1

Um ein Ding zu verstehen, ist es nötig zu erkennen, dass es in vielen (oder womöglich in allen) Teilen ähnlich oder gar gleich ist, Dingen oder Teilen, die bekannt sind.

11 Coherence

{II:29}

Notes for Coherence

Even without a shared content coherence may be direct if the *purpose* is held in common.

IV.[10] Coherence through partial sameness of components

V. Degrees of coherence III 2 & 3

The technique of musical joining[11]

Attention! Make further use of the earlier examples

Appendix: several analyses

Similarity means: partial identity, partial difference

{II:30}

(sonority)
The *tone* has the following characteristics: pitch, duration, color, dynamic

It can become either higher or lower, last briefly or long, have various colors and dynamic shadings.

Rhythm

Duration in music is a characteristic of *sonority and tone*

{ON COHERENCE AND COMPREHENSIBILITY}[12]

{II:35}[13]

Understanding = Recognition of Similarity

§1

To understand a thing, it is necessary to recognize that in many (or, if possible, in all) of its parts, it may be similar or even identical to things or parts that are familiar.

---

10. The sheet containing roman numeral III is apparently lost.

11. Schoenberg discusses "joining technique" more fully in a late manuscript, "The Kinds of Construction of a Phrase": see Christensen and Christensen, *Literary Legacy*, 41.

12. Schoenberg's major essays on coherence and comprehensibility appear later in Schoenberg, "Der musikalische Gedanke und die Logik, Technik und Kunst seiner Darstellung," 55–56, 65–66, 67, 68, 73, 133–43.

13. Pages 35–39 are simultaneously numbered 1–5.

Wenn ich diesen Satz, meinen folgenden Betrachtung{en} zugrunde lege, so meine ich nicht, dass damit endgültig und vollständig gesagt ist, was Verstehen ist, sondern es verhält sich so:

Ein Schrank soll aufgesperrt werden, zu dem der unbekannte Schlüssel nicht vorhanden ist. Man sucht, ehe man sich an den Schlosser wendet — da {man} alle Schlösser mit einem Schlüssel sperrt — alle, die es im Haus giebt, zusammen. Eine Anzahl die bestimmt viel zu gross oder viel zu klein sind, werden sofort, ohne erst zu probieren, ausgeschaltet. Der erste den man für möglich hält, ist zu gross, der nächste zu klein: es war nicht vergeblich, denn nun hat man eine annähernde Vorstellung von der Grösse. Der nächste eine ganz

{II:36}

falsche Form. Man versucht als vierten einen von anderer Form. Schliesslich lauter solche und findet endlich einen, den man ganz umdrehen kann, — der aber doch nicht öffnet. Aber nun kennt man beiläufig das Schloss und hat soviele Schlüssel ausgeschieden, dass nur mehr eine kleine Zahl übrig bleibt. Meist muss man trotz dieser Mühe auf den Schlosser warten; hie und da aber findet sich so der richtige Schlüssel oder man erlernt, wie man einen ähnlichen zurecht feilen muss, damit er sperrt.

Nichts anderes bezweckt meine Voraussetzung: Ob mein Schlüssel passt, ob er sich drehen lassen,[3] ob er sperren wird: man weiss es noch nicht.

Aber ich will es versuchen: vielleicht lernt man das Schloss kennen.

---

§2

Wenn ein Mensch verstehen soll, was ein anderer zu ihm spricht, so ist die erste Voraussetzung dafür, dass der Sprechende

{II:37}

der Sprechende {sic} sich zur Darstellung solcher Zeichen oder Ausdrucksmittel bedient, die dem ersteren bekannt sind, z. Bsp. also die Wörter einer ihm bekannten Sprache. Und der erste Grad des Verstehens tritt hier ein, indem der Zuhörer die bekannten Wörter erkennt. Es müssen nun aber weiterhin auch diese Wörter in einer solchen Reihenfolge und einem solchen Zusammenhang einander folgen, wie es der Sprachgebrauch verlangt. Aber auch die Begriffe und Bedeutungen dieser Wörter müssen — Abweichungen müssten sonst erläutert werden — auf bekannte Art in Beziehung gesetzt sein (es wäre — vom Dadaisten

---

3. läßt.

If I base this statement upon my ensuing observation, I do not mean that it states conclusively and completely what understanding is. Rather, it is as though:

{II:36}

A wardrobe is supposed to be opened, but the unknown key to it is not at hand. Before resorting to the locksmith, one gathers up all the keys in the house, since all locks require a key. A number of keys that are definitely much too large or much too small are immediately excluded, without even trying them out. The first that seems possible is too large, the next too small: yet all was not in vain, because one now has an approximate idea of the size. The next has a completely wrong shape. One tries a differently shaped fourth key. Finally, after {trying} many {keys}, one is found that, although it can be completely turned in the lock, still does not work. Now, however, one knows the lock somewhat, and has rejected so many keys that only a small number are left. Despite this effort it is usually necessary to wait for the locksmith, but now and then the right key can be found in this way, or one may learn how a similar key must be filed so it might lock.

There is no further purpose to my hypothesis: whether my key fits, whether it can be turned, or whether it will lock is not yet known.

All the same, I shall attempt it: perhaps one will become familiar with the lock.

§2

If a person is meant to understand what another is saying to him, the first presupposition is that

{II:37}

the speaker use such signs or means of expression as are known to the listener; for example, the words of a language familiar to him. And the first degree of understanding begins here as the listener recognizes familiar words. In addition, though, these words must succeed each other in such a sequence and context as usage requires. Yet the concepts and meanings of these words must be placed in relation to one another in familiar ways, too, otherwise deviations would have to be explained. (It

darf man hier wohl absehen — z.Bp undenkbar zu sagen: das Kochsalz schreit in hochgeschwungenen Runzeln). Und so geht es weiter{,} bis zum Gedanken, welcher wieder erst verstanden werden kann, wenn erkennbar ist, dass seine einzelnen Teile Bekanntem ähneln oder gleichen.

§3

{II:38} Denn was tut man, wenn man befürchten muss, ein Gedanke sei schwer fasslich, oder schwerfasslich dargestellt, man gestellt[4] man bringt ein Gleichnis. Und das beruht auf Folgendem:
Vergleichen heisst zwar nicht Gleichsetzen, sondern Aehnlichsetzen, d. h. ein Teil der Eigenschaften oder Teile ist gleich, der Rest ungleich. Verglichen aber werden Dinge hinsichtlich ihrer gleichen Teile, während man von den ungleichen für die Dauer des Vergleichs absehen kann, dass es nun aber zwischen dem Gedanken und dem Gegenstand des Vergleiches eine Ähnlichkeit (ohne welche der Vergleich undenkbar ist) giebt, bewirkt, dass {es} in dem im Uebrigen sonst eventuell durchaus neuen Gedanken eine Anzahl von Teilen, Eigenschaften oder dgl. giebt, die auch in einem anderen schon bekannten Gedanken, Vorgang oder dgl. vorkommen, also bekannt sind.
Wie verhält es sich nun mit den übrigbleibenden Teilen?

{II:49 [*sic*]} 1. *Verstehen* beruht auf der Fähigkeit die Ähnlichkeit der Bestandteile mit Bekanntem zu erkennen
2. Dieses *Erkennen der Ähnlichkeit* hat zur Voraussetzung {*sic*} die Fähigkeit des Gedächtnisses: sich die neuen und alten Bestandteile zu merken.
3.

{I:1} *Die Lehre vom Zusammenhang* (Zshg)
Wenn von Dingen gesprochen wird deren Wesen uns gut bekannt ist, so sind wir leicht imstande auch rasch an die mit ihnen zusammenhängenden, von ihnen abgeleiteten, zu ihnen gehörigen Dinge, Tätigkeiten, Zustände und Begriffe zu denken.
Ist. z. B. von einem Besen die Rede so kann ich an seine Stange, an sein Material, ans Kehren, daran dass er neu oder alt und dgl. denken.

---

4. "Man gestellt" is extraneous to this sentence. Schoenberg most likely wrote these words but then changed his thought.

15 *Coherence*

would be inconceivable — the Dadaist may here be disregarded — to say that table salt screams in high-swung wrinkles.) And so it continues up to the idea, which again can only be understood if it is recognizable that its individual parts are identical to or resemble what is familiar.

§3

As it is, what does one do when one is afraid that an idea may be difficult to comprehend or presented in a way that is difficult to comprehend?

{11:38}   One uses a comparison, and this is based on the following:

To compare does not mean to equate but to set up similarly. In other words, a part of the characteristics or of the parts is identical, the rest unlike. Things, however, are compared with regard to their identical parts, while, for the duration of the comparison, one can disregard the unlike parts. That there is, nevertheless, a similarity between the idea and the object of the comparison (without which the comparison is inconceivable) yields the following: in the idea, which possibly may be entirely new, there are a number of parts, characteristics, or the like that occur, too, in another, already familiar idea, event, or the like, {and} that hence are familiar.

How is it, though, with the remaining parts?

{11:49 [*sic*]}   1.   *Understanding* is based on the capacity to recognize the similarity among the components to things that are familiar.
2.   The presupposition for this *recognition of similarity* is the capacity of memory: to remember the new and old components.
3.

{1:1}   *Theory of Coherence* (Coh.)

Whenever there is discussion of things whose nature is very familiar to us, we are able to think easily and quickly of the things, activities, circumstances, and concepts related to them, derived from them, and associated with them.

For example, if a broom is talked about, I can think of its handle, its material, of sweeping, whether it is old or new, and the like.

Ist von Alkohol die Rede, so denk ich an Wein, Bier, Schnaps, an den Rausch, an den Geschmack etc. Soll jedoch an die chemische Zusammensetzung gedacht werden, so ist dieser Gedanke nur dem zugänglich, der das nötige Wissen hat.

Spräche man aber von einer Substanz deren chemische Zusammensetzung unbekannt ist, so wäre niemand imstande mit der Nennung dieser Substanz eine chemische Formel zu associieren.

Es kann also gesagt werden, dass als zusammenhängend mit einem Gegenstand oder Begriff diejenigen Gegenstände und Begriffe empfunden werden, deren Beziehung zu dem Begriff oder Gegenstand uns (unabhängig davon ob es ihn wirklich giebt und ob es nicht mehr solche giebt) *bekannt* ist.[5]

(zu "*Fasslichkeit*"{ })

{1:20}

1.)

Zshg. den folgenden Untersuchungen und Behauptungen liegt die Frage zugrunde:

Wodurch stehen die Töne einer Tonfolge miteinander im Zusammenhang?

Diese Frage soll dann weiter ausgedehnt werden:

Wie *hängen die eine Tonfolge teilenden Phrasen untereinander und mit den sie begleitenden Räumen (Harmonie etc) zusammen? Wie die Phrasen einer Periode eines Satzes? Wie die Sätze untereinander?* u.s.w

—— o ——

16/IV.1917

2.)

I.   *Grundsatz*   (erkennbar: Dinge, Begriffe etc)

Zwei Gedanken haben Zusammenhang, wenn in dem einen ein Teil des andern enthalten ist.

II. der Zusammenhang ist stärker

    a) je wichtigere (wesentlichere) Teile ⎫
    b) je mehr und {ev}wesentl. Teile ⎬ gemeinsam sind
    ⎭

---

5. *bekannt* sind.

If alcohol is mentioned, I think of wine, beer, schnapps, of intoxication, of the taste, etc. If, however, its chemical composition is to be considered, this idea is accessible only to someone with the necessary knowledge.

But if the topic were a substance whose chemical composition is unknown, no one would be able to associate a chemical formula with the name of this substance.

It can thus be stated that coherence is perceptible to us between an object or concept and those objects or concepts whose relation to the stated object or concept is *known* to us (regardless of whether this {object or concept} really exists, and regardless of whether there are no other such objects or concepts).

(In connection with *"Comprehensibility"*)

{1:20}

1.)

Coh. Underlying the following inquiries and statements is the question:

By what means do the tones of a tone sequence cohere with one another?

This question should then be expanded further:

How do the phrases sharing a sequence of notes cohere with each other and with {those in the} spaces (harmony, etc.) accompanying them? How about the phrases of a period, of a sentence? How do the sentences relate to each other? etc.

— o —

16/IV.1917

2.)

I.   *Principle*   (recognizable: things, concepts, etc.)
Two ideas cohere if one of them contains a part of the other.

II.   The relationship is stronger {if}
  a) the more important (more essential) parts } are held in common
  b) the more and possibly essential parts

3.)

Der in zwei Dingen vorhandene Zusammenhang kann durch die Verbindung auffällig oder unauffällig werden.

4.)

Von dem Grade, in welchem vorhandene wesentliche oder unwesentliche Gemeinsamkeiten auffällig oder unauffällig benützt oder herausgearbeitet sind, hängt die *Fasslichkeit* ab.

Sie kann auf ein Minimum reduciert werden, wenn dem Darstellenden das Auffassungsvermögen seiner Zuhörer wenig Sorge macht, sie

{1:21}

muss bis zum äussersten angestrebt werden, wenn der Autor sich an viele oder beschränkte Zuhörer wendet.

5.)

Mann kann unterscheiden zwischen
1. Gedanken, die viele und bedeutende Gemeinsamkeiten haben, welche in[6] auffällig dargestellt sind.
2. Gedanke{n} die wenige aber bedeutende Gemeinsamkeiten haben, welche auffällig dargestellt sind.
3. Solche die viele, teils bedeutende, teils unbedeutende Gemeinsamkeiten haben, welche auffällig dargestellt sind.
4. Solche, die viele{,} aber unbedeutende Gemeinsamkeiten haben, welche auffällig dargestellt sind.
5. Solche, die wenige und unbedeutende Gemeinsamkeiten haben, welche auffällig dargestellt sind.
6.7.8.9.10. Dieselben Gedanken, aber in unauffälliger Darstellung des Gemeinsamen.

— o —

6.)

Für die *Bedeutsamkeit der gemeinsamen Teile* wird sich 1) nicht immer ein absoluter Maßtab finden lassen. 2) wird dieser Maßtab selbst im Laufe der Ereignisse seine Bedeutung ändern, ja verlieren können.

Bsp. zu 1. In der Fremde einen Landsmann zu treffen gehört zu den allgemeingültigen Erfreulichkeiten. Sie wird aber für den, der aus der

---

6. This "in" is extraneous.

19 Coherence

3.)

The coherence existing between two things can become conspicuous or inconspicuous through {their} connection.

4.)

Comprehensibility depends on the degree to which the essential or inessential features held in common are conspicuously or inconspicuously used or worked out.

It can be reduced to a minimum if the performer is little concerned with his listeners' capacities of comprehension;

{1:21}

it must be striven for to the utmost degree if the author addresses himself to many listeners or to those of limited capacity.

5.)

One can distinguish between
1. Ideas that have many and important features in common, which are conspicuously presented.
2. Ideas that have few but important features in common, which are conspicuously presented.
3. Those having numerous, partly important, partly unimportant features in common, which are conspicuously presented.
4. Those that have many but unimportant features in common, which are conspicuously presented.
5. Those that have few and insignificant features in common, which are conspicuously presented.
6.7.8.9.10. The same ideas, but in an inconspicuous presentation of their common {features}

— o —

6.)

For the *significance of the parts held in common*: 1) an absolute standard cannot always be found; 2) in the course of events, this standard will change its significance, or may even lose it.

Ex. for 1. Meeting a fellow countryman abroad is one of the generally accepted pleasures. But it will be embarrassing for the person who was

gemeinsamen Heimat aus unsauberen Gründen fort musste{,} peinlich. Sie kann aber auch für einen peinlich sein, der sich freiwillig selbst[7] verbannt hat.

{1:22}

Bsp. zu 2. Man schliesst sich dem in der Fremde gefundenen Landsmann an, weil man sich einsam fühlt. Nach einiger Zeit aber wird er zudringlich und beansprucht Vertraulichkeit wegen der gemeinsamen Heimat, die man aber nicht gewähren mag.

7.)
Die feineren und die gröberen Zusammenhänge

Man kann unterscheiden zwischen

a) *scheinbar unbedeutenden* Zusammenhängen, die aber auf einem gewissen Niveau *sehr wirksam* sind, und

b) *scheinbar bedeutenden* Zusammenhängen, die unter Umständen *wirkungslos sind*.

8.)
Wie können die vorhandenen Zusammenhänge herausgearbeitet werden? u.s.w. durch welche Mittel

a) auffällig

b) unauffällig   ?

9.)
In welchen Fällen wird man die Zusammenhänge unterstreichen, in welchen verschleiern{?}

10.)
Auf Grund 1/4–5 kann man sagen: Zshg beruht auf Wiederholung, da Teile von A sich in B, C usw. wiederholen. Und:

Zshg entsteht, wenn Teile die teils gleich, teils ungleich sind, so verbunden werden, dass die gleichen hervortreten.

Gegensatz (beziehungsvoller) beruht ebenfalls auf Zusammenhang insofern{,} als die selben Teile wie oben aber so verbunden werden, dass die ungleichen überwiegend auffallen.

Veränderung und Variation beruhen auf Wiederholung insofern, als sowohl einige der gleichen, als auch einige der ungleichen Teile sichtbar

---

7. selbst freiwillig.

obliged to leave his country for unsavory reasons. It can also be embarrassing, though, for someone who voluntarily has gone into exile.

Ex. for 2. One joins the fellow countryman found abroad because of feeling lonely. But after some time he becomes
intrusive and claims familiarity because of common homeland; a familiarity, however, that one does not wish to acknowledge.

7.)
Subtler and rougher connections

One can distinguish between

a) *apparently unimportant* connections that are nevertheless *very effective* at a certain level, and

b) *apparently important* connections that under certain circumstances *are ineffective.*

8.)

How can the existing connections be worked out? Specifically, by what means

a) conspicuously

b) inconspicuously   ?

9.)

In which instances will one underline or veil the connections?

10.)

On the basis of 1/4–5,[14] one may say: coherence is based on repetition, inasmuch as parts of A recur in B, C, etc. And:

Coherence comes into being when parts that are partly the same, partly different, are connected so that those parts that are the same become prominent.

Contrast (relational) is likewise based on coherence, insofar as the same parts as mentioned above are connected so that the unlike parts predominantly attract attention.

Change and variation are based on repetition, insofar as several of the like parts as well as several of the dissimilar parts become discernible.

---

14. 1/4–5: 23–25.

werden. Entwicklung ist eine solche Folge zusammenhängender Ideen, bei welcher ungleiche Teile von anfänglich untergeordneter Bedeutung allmählich zur Hauptsache werden.

{I:4}
 Welches sind die Bedingungen
a) des *Fasslichen*
b) des *musikalisch-Fasslichen*{?}

 a) *Fasslich* ist etwas dann, wenn das *Ganze überblickbar* ist und aus *Theilen besteht* die untereinander und zum Ganzen keine zu fer{n}liegenden Beziehungen (oder besser solche Beziehungen haben, dass sie dem Geiste des Beschauers verständlich sind) und wenn die Anordnung dieser Teile so ist, dass die Beziehung untereinander und zum Ganzen nicht verloren geht.

      Wann ist etwas *überblickbar*?
 Wenn es für unseren Sinn (Auge, etc.) weder zu gross noch zu klein ist oder wenn die *Gliederung* entsprechend ist[8]

{I:6}
 Von Gliederung wird man nur dann sprechen können, wenn die Teile, welche sich von einem Ganzen absondern, abheben, aus ihm herauswachsen und von ihm ausgehen und dennoch festen Zusammenhang mit ihm wahren, wenn also diese Teile sich aus demselben Grunde so zum Ganzen verhalten, aus dem sich z.Bsp. die *Glieder unseres Körpers* zu unserem Körper verhalten; nämlich: sie sondern sich ab um *besondere Funktionen auszuüben.*

 Ist ein musikalisches Stück *so gegliedert*{,} so wird das seine Fasslichkeit erhöhen, weil die einzelnen Glieder an sich verständlich sind.
 Frage:
 Auf welche Art ist eine solche Gliederung musikalisch denkbar &boxed;A ?
A? bedeutet: muss noch beantwortet werden.

     — o —

{I:4}
 Beziehungen von Teilen zum Ganzen und untereinander liegen nahe, wenn wenigstens eine der wesentlichsten im anderen enthalten ist.
 Liegen ferne, wenn nur solche der unwesentlichsten gegenseitig enthalten sind.

---

8. In the original manuscript the text reads "oder bei *entsprechender Gliederung* — siehe Seite 6." After skipping to p.6, Schoenberg fashions the new ending to the sentence transcribed above.

Development is one such succession of related ideas, in which unlike parts, initially subordinate in importance, gradually become the main idea.

{1:4}

What are the requirements of:
a) the *comprehensible*
b) the *musically comprehensible*?

a) Something is *comprehensible* if the *whole is surveyable* and *consists of parts* that have relationships not too remote from each other and from the whole (or better still, that have such relationships as are comprehensible to the mind of the viewer), and if the arrangement of these parts is such that their relationship to each other and to the whole is not lost.

<u>When is something *surveyable*?</u>

If it is neither too large nor too small for our sense perception (eyes, etc.) or if the {structural} *articulation* is appropriate.

{1:6}[15]

One can speak *of articulation* only if the parts that separate from a whole and that stand out, grow out of it, and emanate from it nevertheless maintain a secure connection with it. If these parts then behave the same way toward the whole as, for ex., *our limbs* behave toward our body, {then} namely, they separate in order to *fulfill special functions*.

If a musical piece is *articulated in this way*, its comprehensibility will be increased because the individual components are understandable in themselves.

Question:
In what way is such an articulation musically conceivable $\boxed{A}$?[16]
A? means: still needs to be answered

—— o ——

{1:4}

Relationships of parts to the whole and to one another are close at hand when at least one of the most essential parts is contained in the other.

They are remote if the most inessential parts alone are mutually contained.

---

15. In the manuscript this portion of text appears as an insertion on p.6.

16. "A?" stands for *Antwort?* (answer?). Schoenberg never returned to this question.

24 *Zusammenhang*

Beispiel:
Ein Ganzes G bestünde aus den Teilen
A – B – C – D – E {und}

{1:5}

der Teil A besteht aus a b c f g
    " B "   " a c g d e
    " C "   " a b c e
    " D "   " a f g
    " E "   " f g e

dann besteht auch das Ganze aus a b c d e f g und die Teile haben gute Beziehungen untereinander.

Ist nun die Anordnung so, dass die Beziehung auf das verbindende Teilstück in die Augen springt, so erhöht das die Fasslichkeit{,}

z. Bsp. wenn Teil A a b c f g a hiesse und ihm B folgte, der auch mit a begänne.

(Beispiel für *Schwerfassliches*)!!

Musikalisch-Fasslich ist ein musikalischer Inhalt dann, wenn seine kleinsten und kleinen Bestandtheile (*Perioden, Sätze, Phrasen, Motive*{)}} untereinander und mit dem Ganzen einen solchen Zusammenhang haben, wie es für das Fassliche im Allgemeinen gefordert würde.

Da sich als der kleinste Teil (kleinste gemeinschaftl. Masse) eines musikalischen Stückes dessen *Motiv* herausstellt, so wird im Allgemeinen das Vorkommen dieses kleinsten Teiles in jedem grösseren als Unterpfand für das Zustandekommen von Fasslichkeit gelten dürfen.

Was ist ein Motiv?

{ON MOTIVE AND RHYTHM}

{1:6}
Was ist ein Motiv

25 Coherence

Example:
If a whole, G, consisted of parts
A – B – C – D – E, {and}

{1:5}
    part A consists of a b c f g
    " B " " a c g d e
    " C " " a b c e
    " D " " a f g
    " E " " f g e

then the whole also consists of a b c d e f g, and the parts have good relationships with each other.

Now if the arrangement is such that the relationship to the connecting part is obvious, then comprehensibility is increased.

for ex., if part A were a b c f g a and if B, which also began with a, followed it.

(Example for *something difficult to comprehend*)!!

A musical content is *musically comprehensible* if its smallest and small components (*periods, sentences, phrases, motives*) share such coherence among each other and with the whole as would in general be required for comprehensibility.

Since the *motive* turns out to be the smallest part (smallest common denominator) of a piece of music, in general the presence of this smallest part in every larger part may guarantee that comprehensibility will be achieved.

What is a motive?

{ON MOTIVE AND RHYTHM}[17]

{1:6}
    What is a motive

---

17. For other definitions and comments on motive, see Schoenberg, "Der musikalische Gedanke und die Logik, Technik und Kunst seiner Darstellung," 42; idem, *Fundamentals*, 8; idem, *Models for Beginners in Composition*, 15; idem, *Theory of Harmony*, 34; idem, "Zur Terminologie der Formenlehre" (For a terminology of the "Instruction in form"), Mus 66a–c at the Arnold Schoenberg Institute. For comments on rhythm, see idem, "Der musikalische Gedanke und die Logik, Technik und Kunst seiner Darstellung," 13–14, 184–87.

26 *Zusammenhang*

Es wird gut sein, das so auszuführen, dass der Unterschied zwischen Motor u. Motiv in die Augen springt.

!!

{1:7}

Ein Motiv ist etwas das zu einer Bewegung Anlass giebt. *Eine Bewegung ist jene Veränderung eines Ruhezustandes, die ihn in sein Gegenteil verkehrt.* Man kann somit das Motiv mit einer treibenden Kraft vergleichen. Eine solche wird eines Gegenstandes bedürfen, auf den sie wirkt.
Sie wird gross genug sein müssen um Diesen aus seinem Ruhezustand zu bringen und die Bewegung, die sie erweckt wird ihrer Grösse{,} Dauer und Art nach abhängen von der Art der treibenden Kraft und des getriebene Gegenstandes.

—— x ——

Das Vorhergehende ist wohl nicht ganz richtig: Was eine Bewegung hervorruft ist ein *Motor*. Man muss zwischen *Motor* und *Motiv* unterscheiden.

Das *Motiv* wird folgendermassen zu definieren sein{:}

Als Motiv ist ein Ding dann zu bezeichnen, wenn es bereits *unter der Wirkung einer treibenden Kraft steht, ihren Impuls bereits empfangen hat und im Begriff ist, ihm Folge zu leisten.* Es ist vergleichbar mit einer Kugel auf einer schiefen Ebene im Augenblick bevor sie fortrollt; mit einem befruchteten Samen; mit einem zum Schlag erhobene Arm etc.

Welches sind daher *musikalisch die Eigenschaften eines Motives*{?}

Vorher: jedes *kleinste musikalische Ereignis* kann zum Motiv werden, wenn man es wirken lässt, der einzelne Ton bereits kann Folgen haben.

13/4.1917   Jeder *einzelne Ton* kann unter Umständen Motiv sein; z.Bsp. Beethoven op.59 – 1, Seite 5

   etc.   die halbe Note ist Motiv dieser Stelle.

27 Coherence

!!

{1:7}

A motive is something that gives rise to a motion. *A motion is that change in a state of rest which turns it into its opposite.* Thus, one can compare the motive with a driving force. Such a driving force will require an object on which it acts.

This driving force will have to be great enough to bring the object out of its condition of rest; and the motion it causes will depend for its size, duration, and kind on the type of driving force and on the object driven.

It will be good to carry this out, so as to make obvious the difference between motor and motive.[18]

—— x ——

The preceding is probably not entirely correct: What causes motion is a *motor*. One must distinguish between *motor* and *motive*.

A *motive* may be defined as follows:

A thing is termed *a motive if it is already subject to the effect of a driving force, has already received its impulse, and is on the verge of reacting to it.* It is comparable to a sphere on an inclined plane at the moment before it rolls away; to a fertilized seed; to an arm raised to strike, etc.

What, therefore, are the *musical characteristics of a motive?*

First of all: even *the smallest musical event* can become a motive; if {it is} permitted to have an effect, even an individual tone can carry consequences.

13/4.1917   Under certain circumstances, each *single tone* can be a motive; for ex., Beethoven, op.59, no.1, page 5[19]

 etc.   The half note is the motive of this passage.

---

18. Compare Schoenberg, *Theory of Harmony*, 34.

19. See mm.144–45 or 146–47.

28 *Zusammenhang*

{I:8}   Aber ein einzelner Ton könnte auch *zu Anfang* eines Gedankens stehen und allein dessen Motiv sein.

Denn ohne weiteres hingestellt, *stellt er bereits eine Frage*: die nach seiner harmonischen Bedeutung (ist er Terz, Quint, Grundton etc?)

Mann könnte genötigt werden diese Frage zu beantworten, also fortzusetzen — und somit hat er diese Bewegung veranlasst.

Besser erkennt man die Wirkung eines Motivs bereits, wenn es eine *Tonfolge* ist. In diesem Fall hat es auch bereits *Ryt{h}mus*.

{I:9}   Die rein musikalische Charakteristik ist dann gegeben 1. durch die Notenwerte und ihr Verhältnis zum Takt, 2. durch die Anzahl der vorkommenden Töne, 3. durch die Intervalle. (Auf höheren Stufen treten dann noch dazu der Ausdruck, Charakter, Dynamik (?) und eventuell die zugrundeliegende Harmonie oder andere damit verbundene Stimmen.

Jedes in einem Musikstück durch (eventuell veränderte, variierte) Wiederholungen wirkende kleinste Teilchen ist je nach den Umständen als Motiv anzusehen.

| *Definition* | Musikalisches Motiv ist eine tönende ryt{h}misierte Erscheinung, welche

{I:10}   durch ihre (eventuell variierten) Wiederholungen im Verlaufe eines Musikstückes den Anschein zu erwecken vermag, als ob sie dessen Material sei.

—— o ——

In diesem Sinn hat z.Bsp. eine Begleitungsfigur ein Motiv, sie kann auch mehrere haben

29 Coherence

{1:8}

But an individual tone could also stand *at the beginning* of an idea and by itself be its motive.

Because, without further ado, an *individual tone immediately poses a question* concerning its harmonic significance (is it a third, fifth, fundamental, etc.?)

One might be obliged to answer this question, thereby to continue asking it; consequently, the tone has caused this motion.

The effect of a motive is more readily understood if it is *a succession of tones*. In this case, it is already endowed with *rhythm* as well.

{1:9}[20]

The purely musical characteristic is then given 1. by the note values and their relationship to the bar, 2. by the number of occurring tones, 3. by the intervals. (At more advanced levels there are additionally: expression, character, dynamics (?)[21] and possibly the underlying harmony or other voices connected with it.

Depending on the circumstances, each smallest part that is active in a piece of music through (possibly changed {or} varied) repetitions is to be regarded as a motive.

 boxed:Definition   A musical motive is a sounding, rhythmicized phenomenon that,

{1:10}

by its (possibly varied) repetitions in the course of a piece of music, is capable of creating the impression that it is the material of the piece.

— o —

In this sense, for example, an accompanimental figure can be based on a motive, but it may also be based on several.

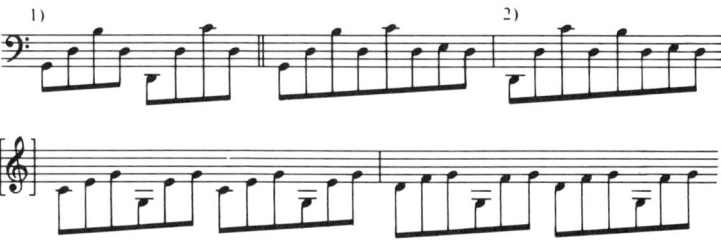

---

20. In the manuscript this portion of text appears as an insertion on p.9.

21. Schoenberg never explains this question mark.

30 *Zusammenhang*

Das wichtigste Merkmal eines Motivs ist seine Wiederholung.
An den Wiederholungen erkennt man das Vorhandensein eines Motivs.

— o —

// Frage: ist eine Erscheinung, die sich *nicht wiederholt kein* Motiv???
Antwort: das kann ein Motiv sein, das sich (einstweilen) nicht wiederholt; oder eine Kette mehrerer (auch dasjenige das dann kommt) Motive, von denen ein einzelnes sich wiederholt.

— o —

{I:8} *Was ist Rhyt{h}mus?*
Rhyt{h}mus ist die in *messbaren Zeitabständen erfolgende Wiederholung einer Bewegung.* Unterbrechung eines Ruhezustandes

Beim musikalischen Rhyt{h}mus werden die Zeitabstände meist einfach, durch 2, 3 oder 4 teilbare (oder vielfache der kleinsten Einheit), der Bewegungen{,} Klänge oder Schälle sein. Meist tritt dann noch die *Betonung* dazu, welche einzelnen (gewöhnlich regelmässig, z.Bsp. jeder 2., 3., 4., auch 5. 6. 7. 8. oder 9). Wiederholungen beigegeben ist. Eigentlich ensteht der höhere kunstmässige Rhyt{h}mus erst durch diese Betonungen. Es werden durch sie eine (im allgemeinen gleichbleibende) Zahl von Wiederholungen zu Takten zusammengefasst. Und das eigentlich musikalisch-rhyt{h}mische Motiv bedient sich des ihm zugrundeliegenden Rhyt{h}mus (Takt) in der Weise, dass es in regelmässiger oder unregelmässiger Folge betonte und unbetonte, kurze und lange Noten bringt und dazwischen liegendes in
{I:9} Form von Pausen auslässt, oder durch Verbindung mit längerklingendem{,} vorher angeschlagenem{,} unangeschlagen lässt.

Als musikalischer-Rhyt{h}mus wird also eine tönende oder klingende Erscheinung zu bezeichnen sein, die aus kurzen und langen, betonten und unbetonten Anschlägen besteht, denen einen genau abgemessene Zeitteilung, der Takt, zugrunde liegt.

Im einfachsten Sinn ist dann jede Wiederholung gleicher Noten bereits ein musikalischer Rhyt{h}mus z.Bsp.

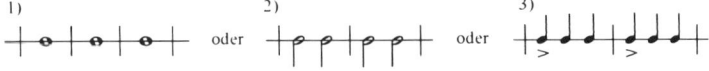

31 Coherence

The most important characteristic of a motive is its repetition.
The presence of a motive can be recognized by the repetitions.

— o —

// Question: is a phenomenon which is *not repeated* *not* a motive???
Answer: A motive can be that which (for the present) is not repeated; or a chain of several motives (including the one that here occurs) a single one of which is repeated.

— o —

{1:8}

What is rhythm?
Rhythm is the *repetition of a motion occurring in measurable time intervals.* Interruption of a state of rest

With musical rhythm, time intervals of the motions, sonorities, or sounds are most often simply divisible by 2, 3, or 4 (or by multiples of the smallest unit). Customarily, there is also an *accentuation* that is assigned to individual repetitions, ({occurring} regularly, for example, every 2d, 3d, 4th, also 5th, 6th, 7th, 8th, or 9th). Actually, high artistic rhythm comes into being only by means of these accentuations, through which a number of repetitions (in general, constant ones) are grouped into measures. And the true musical-rhythmic motive makes use of its underlying rhythm (meter) so that it presents, in regular or irregular sequence, notes that are accented and unaccented, short and long, and omits, in

{1:9}

the form of rests, whatever is in between them; or else leaves notes unattacked by connecting them with longer, previously attacked ones.

Thus, musical rhythm can be termed a sounding or resonating phenomenon, consisting of short and long, accented and unaccented attacks, which are based on a precisely measured division of time, the bar.

In the simplest sense, then, every repetition of notes of equal value is a musical rhythm, e.g.,

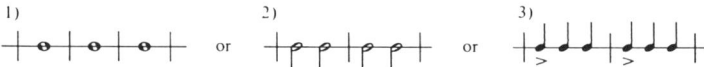

insbesondere dann, wenn die verschiedenen Anschläge in einem verschiedenen Verhältnis zum betonten Taktteil stehen, wie z.Bsp. 2) u. 3).

Höher organisierte *Rhyt{h}men* sind solche von abwechslungsreicherer Gestalt etc. —

— o —

{ON PRINCIPLES OF STRUCTURE}

{I:14}

Gliederung

Eine zweckmässige Gliederung wird *Haupt- und Nebensachen auseinanderhalten*, indem sie jedem seinen richtigen Platz, Länge, Gewicht, Form etc. giebt.

Was sind musikalisch *Haupt- und Nebensachen*?

Um das zu beantworten, ist es nötig nach der Bestimmung eines Tonstückes zu fragen.

Ein Meister-Komponist hat immer eine klare Vorstellung davon, was sein Stück werden, wie lang und welchen Charakter es haben soll. Er weiss, wann er ein kurzes Klavierstück, wann ein Streichquartett und wann er eine grosse Symphonie schreiben wird. Genauso wie ein Baumeister weiss, ob er eine Villa oder ein Schloss baut.

Das Werk ist also für ihn, noch ehe es in allen Details ausgeführt ist, bereits *bestimmt*. Er hat ein Bild davon *in sich*.

{I:15} Wenn er nun daran geht, dieses Bild zu verwirklichen, so wird er sich bewusst oder unbewusst darüber Rechenschaft geben, welches der auszudrückende Gegenstand {ist}, in welcher Form er darzustellen und wie viel oder wenig{er} über ihn in diesem Fall zu sagen hat. Er wird von einem anfänglich mehr allgemeinen Gefühl je länger er sich mit dieser Arbeit befasst desto mehr zu vollständig klaren Vorstellungen gelangen, bis das Werk in seinen Hauptzügen fertig vor ihm steht.

Das ist wohl in dieser Form nicht wahr, wie ich aus eigener Erfahrung weiss.

especially when the various beats are in a different relation to the accented part of the bar, as for example 2) and 3).

Rhythms of a higher order of organization are those with a richer variety in their makeup, etc. —

—— o ——

{ON PRINCIPLES OF STRUCTURE}

Articulation [22]

A purposeful structuring will distinguish between *main* and *subordinate matters* by giving each its proper place, duration, weight, form, etc.

What are musical *main and subordinate matters*?

To answer that, it is necessary to ask about the purpose of a piece of music.

An accomplished composer always has a clear conception of what his piece should become, of its length, and of its character. He knows when he will write a short piano piece, when a string quartet, and when a large symphony, just as an architect knows whether he is building a house or a castle.

Thus, the work is already *determined* for him even before it is realized in all its details. He possesses an image of it *within himself.*

If he now sets about realizing this image, he will consciously or unconsciously become aware of what the object is intended to express, in what shape he must present it, and how much or how little he may have to say about it in this case. Starting from an initially rather general feeling, the longer he deals with this task, the more he will achieve a completely clear conception until he envisions the finished work in all its main features.

This is probably not true in this form, as I know from my own experience.

---

22. Compare Schoenberg, *Theory of Harmony*, 289; idem, "Der musikalische Gedanke und die Logik, Technik und Kunst seiner Darstellung," 221–27.

Soweit mich nicht bei meinem früheren Schaffen die alten Formen geführt haben, wäre ich auch da nicht imstande gewesen vorher zu sagen, welches die Haupt- und Nebensachen sind. Und was mein Späteres anbelangt, so erinnere ich mich augenblicklich (weiteres fällt mir sicher ein andermal ein), dass ich beim Schluss meiner „glücklichen Hand" zwar eine *sehr genaue* Vorstellung von dem hatte, was ich sagen wollte, sogar schon die wichtigsten Motive notiert hatte und doch nicht hätte sagen können was Haupt- u. Nebensachen sind.

Man darf das nicht vom Künstler aus, sondern muss es vom *Schüler*, *Lehrer* und *Historiker* aus darstellen.

Es ist notwendig hier bewusst die *Schulform* darzustellen. Aber man *muss das sagen, dass es keine Ästhetik ist.*

{1:16}

I) Wenn ein Stück *lang werden* soll so wird es entweder
   a) aus vielen kurzen Teilen oder
   b) aus wenigen grossen " oder
   c) " vielen grossen " bestehen
(die Teile können dann ebenso gehalten sein, die ihrigen dergleichen)

II) Wenn ein *Stück kurz werden* soll so wird es entweder
   a) aus wenigen langen Teilen oder
   b) " " kurzen " "
   c) " nur einem " (oder langen) Teil bestehen.

— o —

{1:31}   18.4.1917

fast jedes Thema erweist sich als Resultierende verschiedener Kräfte. Es wirken mehrere Gesetze gleichzeitig in ihm.
   a) Beispiele dafür
   b) welches sind solche Gesetze

To the extent that the traditional forms did not guide me *in my earlier works*, I would not even have been able to say in advance what the main and subordinate matters were to be. And as for my later work, I recall immediately (further instances will surely occur to me some other time) that at the conclusion of my *Die glückliche Hand*, I indeed had a *very precise* idea of what I wanted to say, had even jotted down the most important motives, and I still could not have said what main and subordinate matters were.

This has to be presented by the <u>student's</u>, the *teacher's* and *historian's* point of view, yet not expected from the artist himself.

It is necessary here consciously to represent the <u>schoolbook-form</u>, but <u>it must be said that this is not aesthetics</u>.

{1:16}

I) If a piece *is supposed to be long*, it will consist either of
    a) many short parts, or
    b) a few large parts, or
    c) many large parts.
(the parts can then be kept at a length like those of their kind)

II) If a piece *is supposed to be short*, then it will consist either of
    a) a few long parts, or
    b) a few short " "
    c) only one short (or long) part.

—— o ——

{1:31}

18.4.1917

Almost every theme proves to be the outcome of various interacting forces. Various laws operate simultaneously in it.
    a) examples for this
    b) which are these laws[23]

---

23. For further comments on theme, see unpublished manuscript Mus 66 at the Arnold Schoenberg Institute; Schoenberg, *Fundamentals*, 101–2; idem, *Style*, 472–73.

{I:10}

— o —

Formbildende Prinzipien

I   Das Prinzip der *Wiederholung*
II   " " " *Veränderung* (Abwechslung)
III   " " " *Entwicklung*
IV   " " des *Gegensatzes*

— o —

Das Motiv *pflanzt sich fort*{,} indem es sich wiederholt, und aus sich neue Gestalten hervorbringt.

{I:11}

Ein Motiv kann auf folgende Arten wiederholt werden:

I. *genau*   1) a) vom gleichen Ton aus
　　　　　　　　b) von einem anderen Ton aus
　　　　　　　　c) mit vollkommen gleichen Intervallen
　　　　　　　　d)   "   relativ   "   "
　　　　　　　　e)   "   veränderten   "   "   (Dur, Moll, etc.)

　　　　　　2) a) im gleichen Rhyt{h}mus
　　　　　　　　b) in der Vergrösserung
　　　　　　　　c)   "   "   Verkleinerung
　　　　　　　　d) in verändertem Rhyt{h}mus (Verzierungen etc)

II. *ungenau*   1) *zufällige* a) in freier Nachahmung der Intervalle (eventuell Umkehrung des ganzen oder einzelner Theile{)}
　　　　　　　　　　　　　　　b) in freier Nachamung der Rhyt{h}men

　　　　　　2) Variationen (formale)
　　　　　　3) Entwickelnde Variationen.

— o —

Die *Wiederholung* ist ein formbildendes Prinzip des Zusammenhanges.

Sie unterliegt der Gefahr{,} *Monotonie* hervorzurufen.

Zu diesem Zwecke wird ein anderes formbildendes Prinzip angewendet:

Coherence

{I:10}

— o —

Structuring Principles[24]

I   The principle of *repetition*
II   "   "   " *change* (variety)
III "   "   " *development*
IV   "   "   " *contrast*

— o —

The motive *reproduces itself* by repeating and engendering new shapes from itself.

{I:11}

A motive can be repeated in the following ways:

I. *exactly*
   1) a) starting from the same tone
       b) starting from a different tone
       c) with identical intervals
       d) " almost the same intervals
       e) " changed intervals (major, minor, etc.)
   2) a) in the same rhythm
       b) in augmentation
       c) in diminution
       d) in altered rhythm (ornaments, etc.)

II. *not exactly*
   1) *by chance* a) in free imitation of the intervals (possibly inversion of the whole or of individual parts)
               b) in free imitation of the rhythms
   2) variations (formal)
   3) developing variations

— o —

Repetition is a structuring principle of coherence.
It is subject to the danger of producing *monotony*.
For this purpose, a different structuring principle is used:

---

24. Principles of repetition, contrast, variation, and development are discussed at length in the opening chapters of *Fundamentals of Musical Composition* and illustrated in the examples throughout *Models for Beginners in Composition*.

38 Zusammenhang

die *Abwechslung*

Es giebt folgende Arten Abwechslung hervorzurufen{:}

- A) Rhyt{h}mische   Änderungen (auch Tempo)
- B) Intervall   "   (Richtung, Grösse)
- C) Harmonische   "
- D) Satz   "
- E) Instrumentations "   { Oberstimme / Unter " / Mittel " }   Gegenstimme etc.
- F) Dynamische   "

{1:12} Man kann *zwei Arten von Variierung* eines Motivs unterscheiden.

Bei der 1. scheinen die Veränderungen meist nur gleichsam *ornamentalen* Zweck zu haben; Sie treten auf um Abwechslung zu schaffen und verschwinden oft wieder spurlos. (selten ohne die 2. Art!!)

die 2. kann man *entwickelnde Variation* nennen. Die Veränderungen gehen mehr oder weniger direkt auf das Ziel los neue Gedanken entspringen zu lassen. (liquidieren abwickelnd)

$$b_1 = b + \frac{a}{2}$$

aus b entwickelt sich b_1 um im 9. Takt dann in einem neuen Thema die Verbindung mit dem vorhergehenden Gedanken herzustellen. Das Bei-

39 Coherence

Variety

The following ways of producing variety are available:

A) rhythmic changes (including tempo)
B) intervallic changes (direction, size)
C) harmonic changes
D) phrase changes
E) changes in the instrumentation $\begin{Bmatrix} \text{upper voice} \\ \text{lower voice} \\ \text{middle voice} \end{Bmatrix}$ counter voice, etc.
F) dynamic changes

{1:12}   One can distinguish *two methods of varying* a motive.

With the first, usually the changes virtually seem to have nothing more than an *ornamental* purpose; they appear in order to create variety and often disappear without a trace. (seldom without the second method!!)

The second can be termed *developing variation*.[25] The changes proceed more or less directly toward the goal of allowing new ideas to arise.   (to liquidate, unravelling[26])

$$b_1 = b + \frac{a}{2}^{27}$$

b_1 develops from b in order to establish in a new theme in bar 9 the connection with the preceding idea. The example is admittedly crude. In

---

25. For comments on developing variation, see Schoenberg, *Style*, 129; idem, *Fundamentals*, 8; idem, *Models*, 15.

26. For definitions of *liquidation*, see Schoenberg, *Theory of Harmony*, 207–8; idem, "Der musikalische Gedanke und die Logik, Technik und Kunst seiner Darstellung," 33–34, 165; idem, *Fundamentals*, 58, 152; idem, *Models*, 16. For definitions of *unraveling*, see Schoenberg, "Der musikalische Gedanke, seine Darstellung und Durchführung," section 4, paragraph 16; idem, *Style*, 290–91.

27. $\frac{a}{2}$ refers to half of the variant of *a* in bar 2.

40 *Zusammenhang*

spiel ist natürlich plump. In Kunstwerken wird etwas eher dazu dienen die $\tfrac{1}{16}$-Bewegung einzuführen. z.Bsp. Mozart C-Dur Str. Quartett, 1. Satz

Das Ziel ist ⊕ $\tfrac{a1}{2}$ eine Sechzehntelfigur die in Terzen aufwärts läuft. Der vorbereitende Schritt dazu geschieht bei x [Eigentlich aber hat auf diesen schon die Viola (auf die Beschleunigung durch den

2 Takte vorher{)} und das Cello (Vergrösserung der Figur) auf den Inhalt vorbereitet.{]}

{1:13}

Die $\tfrac{1}{16}$-Noten der II Gge. lösen die Bewegung aus. Die II Gge. lenkt die Aufmerksamkeit auf sich durch die Imitation im 3 Takt. Sie *und* das betreffende Motiv erhalten dadurch Bedeutung. Darum kann es dann in

works of art, such a thing will more likely serve the purpose of introducing the sixteenth motion.

e.g., Mozart C major String Quartet, 1st movement

The goal is  a sixteenth-note figure that moves upward in thirds. The preparatory step occurs at x, though [actually the viola has already prepared for this (at the acceleration by means of the

2 measures before),[28] and the cello (augmentation of the figure) has already prepared for the content.][29]

The sixteenth notes of the second violin initiate the motion. The second violin calls attention to itself through the imitation in the 3d bar. The second violin *and* the motive in question thus acquire significance. In

---

28. This figure does not occur two measures before in the score.

29. In the score the cello appears in eighth-note rhythm.

42 Zusammenhang

variierter Form im nächsten Takt *Hauptsache* werden ($\frac{1}{16}$ tel Noten). Die Form a1 ist bereits die Form die später gebraucht wird. Die Abwechslung erfordert, dass sie wieder zurücktritt, nachdem sie sich ein wenig in den Vordergrund gedrängt hat. Deshalb die abschweifenden Formen a2 u. a3. Aber im letzten Moment nähert a4 sich a1 wieder ein wenig, damit die Hauptsache nicht vergesse werde.

—— o ——

das ist eines der schönsten Beispiele von entwickelnder Variation.
*siehe unten.
*Im weiteren Verlauf ist dann die Geigenfigur zu beachten.

—— o ——

Auf welche Arten können zwei *Gedanken miteinander verbunden werden*?
A) durch Ueberleitungen (vermittelndes)
B) durch Gegensatz

{1:14}

A *Vermittelndes*:
I. Harmonisch indem
   a) die Tonart (v.) herbeigeführt wird
   b) ein Akkord eingeführt wird{,} der auf das Kommende vorbereitet
II. Motivisch indem
   a) der kommende Ryt{h}mus allmählich entwickelt wird
   b) besonders auffallende Melodieveränderungen (Intervalle) früher angeführt werden

43 Coherence

varied form, the motive can therefore become the *main idea* in the next measure (sixteenth notes). Form a1 is already the form that is used later. Variety requires that it again retreat after having somewhat pushed itself into the foreground. Hence the digressing forms a2 and a3. But at the last moment a4 again approaches a1 somewhat, so that the main idea may not be forgotten.

— o —

This is one of the most perfect examples of developing variation.
* See below.
* In the following {unfolding} one should take note of the violin figure.[30]

— o —

In which ways can two *ideas be connected to one another*?
A) through transitions (mediating)
B) through contrast

{1:14}

A. *Mediating*:
I. Harmonic, in that
   a) the key (v.) is led toward
   b) a chord is introduced that prepares for what is coming
II. Motivic, in that
   a) the subsequent rhythm is gradually developed
   b) especially striking changes of melody (intervals) are brought in earlier

---

30. In the original this sentence and the example to which it refers appears as an insertion at the bottom of p.13.

B. *Gegensatz*
    I. Harmonisch:
    indem der Augenblick vor dem Eintritt so gestellt wird, dass ⎱ das neue Thema überraschend auftritt
    II. Rhyt{h}misch ⎰
    III. durch eine Generalpause

— o —

{1:16}

Die ersten einfachsten formbildenden Prinzipien (formbld. Przp.)
1. Zusammenhaltende
2. Auseinandertreibende
3. Neutrale (Schwebende?)

{1:17}
        (ziehende)
1) *Zusammenhaltende*: Festhalten von Tonart, Takt, Rhyt{h}mus
2) *auseinandertreibende*: Verlassen von Tonart, Takt, Rhyt{h}mus
3) *Neutrale*: (ruhende, schwebende)
Wie wird in einem solchen einstimmigen Sätzchen die Tonart
    a) ausgedrückt
    b) festgehalten
    c) verlassen
    d) wieder hergestellt und befestigt

a) Die Tonart wird ausgedrückt: 1. durch den Grundton (ihn allein anzugeben genügte, wenn ihm nicht durch folgende Töne widersprochen würde) 2. die Quint, 3. die Terz, 4. die VII 5. die IV.) durch 1–5–1, oder 1–7–1 oder 1–2–1 ist die Tonart bereits ausgedrückt; aber nicht unzweideutig. Denn wenn z Bsp nach 1–5–1 folgt 7 6 5 ♯4 5 so kann es Ober-Dominante, wenn 7♭, 6, 5, 4, 3, 2 folgt, Unter Dom. gewesen sein; durch 7 6 7 3 wird III, durch 7♭ 6 8♯ 2 II, durch 4 3 2 5♯ 6 VI möglich.

Die Ausdrücken der Tonart ist meist von Vorteil, da es Geschlossenheit sichert. (Doch kann man auf diesen Vorteil auch verzichten; er ist der natürlichste; ebenso natürlich, wie die Sequenz, aber wer ohne ihre Vorteile auskommen kann, vermag es sich vorzustellen, dass man auch auf die der Tonalität verzichten kann).

Eines der wichtigsten Mittel die Tonart auszudrücken, ist, *ihr nicht zu widersprechen*.

Aus diesem Grunde ist auch *der Schluss die allergeeignetste Stelle dafür*,

B. *Contrast*
  I. Harmonically,
     in that the moment is so positioned prior to its entrance } that the new theme occurs surprisingly
  II. Rhythmically
  III. Through a general pause

— o —

{1:16}   *The first and simplest structural principles* (struc. prin.)
1. binding ones
2. separating ones
3. neutral ones (fluctuating?)

{1:17}   (pulling)
1) *binding ones*: adhering to the key, meter, rhythm
2) *separating ones*: abandonment of key, meter, rhythm
3) *neutral ones*: (static, fluctuating)

In such a short one-voice phrase, how is the key
  a) expressed
  b) adhered to
  c) abandoned
  d) reestablished and strengthened

a) The key is expressed: 1. by means of the fundamental tone (it would suffice to state it alone if it were not to be contradicted by subsequent tones) 2. the fifth, 3. the third, 4. the VII[31] 5. the IV. The key is already expressed by means of 1–5–1, or 1–7–1, or 1–2–1; but not unambiguously. For if (e.g.) 7 6 5 #4 5 follows 1–5–1, it can have been the upper dominant; if 7♭, 6, 5, 4, 3, 2 follows, it can have been the subdominant; it becomes III by means of 7 6 7 3, II by means of 7♭ 6 8# 2, VI is possible by means of 4 3 2 3 5# 6.

Expressing the key is generally advantageous, as it assures unity. (However, one can also forgo this advantage; it is the most natural, just as natural as the sequence; yet anyone who can manage without its advantages may contrive to imagine that one can also forgo tonality).

One of the most important means of expressing the key is *not to contradict it*.

For this reason also, the *conclusion* is *the most appropriate place for it*;

---

31. "VII" is the most likely transcription of this illegible passage.

{I:18}

denn da diejenige Tonart, die das letzte Wort behielt, auch Recht behält, so könnte hier unter Umständen auch ein weniger starker Schluss befriedigen. Dass das so richtig ist, beweisen die Plagialschlüsse, und dass es unrichtig ist{,} beweisen harmonisch misslungene Schlüsse (z.Bsp. bei Schumann) [Interessant in dieser Hinsicht ist der Andante Satz der VIII. Beethoven-das zufällige B-Dur. Mein unbegrenzter Respekt vor Beethoven und da ich ausserdem keinen einzigen Fall bei ihm{,} ausser diesem kenne, zwingen mich anzunehmen, dass dieser ungenügende Schluss irgendeiner Absicht entspreche. Da ich aber diese Absicht bis jetzt nicht herausfinden konnte und immer nur die Unvollständigkeit des Schlusses spüre und sehe, so kann ich doch nur annehmen, dass hier ein Mangel ist.{]}

Ähnlich verhält es *sich mit dem Anfang*: nicht sehr geeignet, die Tonart festzustellen. Aber es giebt viele Fälle der klassischen Literatur, wo von dieser Möglichkeit nicht Gebrauch gemacht wird.

[Die Tonalität (siehe auch meine *Harmonielehre*) ist keine Notwendigkeit eines Tonstückes, sondern eine Möglichkeit. Die alte Aesthetik hält die Tonalität für ein ewiges Gesetz; das ist aber ein Irrtum]

—— o ——

17.IV.1917

Das *Festhalten der Tonart* ist eines der bewährtesten *Formprinzipien*. Es sichert a) *Einheitlichkeit* (in dieser Hinsicht)
b) *Mannigfaltigkeit*.

a) Die *Einheitlichkeit* wird hervorgerufen durch die tonale Wirkung der Uebereinstimmung von Anfang und Schluss und durch die harmonische Beziehung aller abschweifenden Teile auf die Haupttonart.

b) die *Mannigfaltigkeit* wird durch jene harm. Abschweifungen hervorgerufen, die zum Ausdrücken der Tonart nötig sind.

—— o ——

Die Tonart wird angegeben durch eine zweckmässige Folge der

however, since that key which has had the last word remains the right one, under certain circumstances a less strong conclusion might suffice. That this is correct is proved by the plagal

{1:18} cadence, that it may be incorrect is proven by harmonically unsuccessful conclusions (for example, in Schumann). [Interesting in this respect is the Andante[32] movement of Beethoven's Eighth — the coincidental B-flat major. My unbounded respect for Beethoven, and the fact that I know of no single such instance in his music apart from this one, compel me to assume that this unsatisfying conclusion might comply with some intention. But since I have not yet been able to discover this intention and still experience and see only the incompleteness of the ending, I can only assume that there is a shortcoming here.][33]

The case is similar *with beginnings*: not very suited to establishing the key. But there are many cases in the classical literature where no use is made of this possibility {of not establishing the key}.

[Tonality (see also my *Theory of Harmony*) is not a necessity for a piece of music, but rather a possibility. Traditional aesthetics holds tonality to be as an eternal law, but that is an error.][34]

— o —

17.IV.1917

Adherence to the key is one of the most proven *principles of form*. It guarantees a) *uniformity* (in this respect)
  b) *diversity*

a) *Uniformity* is brought about by the tonal effect of the agreement between beginning and end, and by the harmonious relationship between all the digressions and the main key.

b) *Diversity* is brought about by those harmonic digressions necessary for expressing the key.

— o —

The key is indicated by means of an appropriate succession of its

---

32. Allegretto Scherzando.

33. Compare Schoenberg, *Style*, 273.

34. See Schoenberg, *Theory of Harmony*, 394.

48 *Zusammenhang*

{1:19} leitereigenen Töne und leiterfremden in solcher Anordnung, dass die entstehenden Abschweifungen wieder durch Gegenmassregeln gebändigt werden können.

Das wichtigste Mittel zum Ausdrücken, Angeben und Befestigen der Tonart ist die Kadenz. Sie beruht im einstimmig melodischen Satz auf denselben Prinzipien, wie im harmonischen.

Grundsaz: *Ein Ton dem nicht widersprochen wird, steht für die Tonart.*
Daher: *Schlusston drückt an sich die Tonart aus.*

Aber was vorhergeht, darf auch nicht widersprechen, sondern soll unterstützen.

Geeignet vorherzugehen
1) der 5te Ton (deutet v. Stufe an{)}
2) der 2te Ton ("   v. oder vii an und {)}
3) der 7te Ton ("   v.   "   "   {)}
   ist *melodisch* der fallende Leitton. (*Skalateil*)
              "   steigende   "

daher   1. Melodische Kadenz   5. u. 1.
         2.   "   "   2. u. 1.
         3.   "   "   7. u. 1.

Was kann gut vor 5 kommen? der   4. 2. 6. (ev. 3) │ 7?
         "   2   "   "   4. 6.   5?   ║ 7?
         "   7   "   "   2 4? 6. 3?   │ 5

vor 5, der 4. weil IV II Stufe ⎫	vor 2 der 4. weil IV oder II Stufe ⎫
" 2. " II " ⎬ GUT	" 6. " IV II VI " ⎬ GUT
" 6. " IV II od. VI " ⎭	" 3. weil melodisch Skala ⎭
" 3. weniger gut wegen Akkord!	" 5. weil bloss Vertauschung
" 7. bloss Vertauschung "	" 7. " " "

vor 7 der 2. weil II. Stufe ⎫	Was bloss Vertauschung ist, ist nicht
4. weil II.IV.II. (Tritonus) ⎬ GUT	geradezu schlecht, aber doch nur aus rhyt{h}mischen Gründen anzuwenden.
6. weil Skalateil ⎭	
wenig gut{:}	????
3. weil Bestandteil 3.7 der III. nicht unmöglich	
5. weil blosse Vertauschung	

49 Coherence

{1:19}

scale tones, as well as those not belonging to its scale in such an order that

any digressions arising can promptly be brought under control by countermeasures.

The most important means for expressing, stating, and strengthening the key is the cadence. It is based on the same principles in a one-voice melodic phrase as in a harmonic phrase.

Principle: *A tone that is not contradicted represents the key.*

Accordingly: *The concluding tone itself expresses the key.*

But what precedes must also not contradict, but should support.

Suited to precede[35]

1) the 5th tone (indicates the V. degree)
2) the 2nd tone (" V. or VII)
3) the 7th tone (" V. " ")

and *melodically* is the descending leading tone. (*scale segment*)
                is the ascending " "

Accordingly   1. melodic cadence   5 and 1.
               2. melodic cadence   2 and 1.
               3. melodic cadence   7 and 1.

What can best	occur before 5?	4. 2.	6 (possibly 3)	7?
occur before 2?	4. 6.	3.	5?	7?
occur before 7?	2	4? 6.	3?	5

before 5, the 4th because IV II degree ⎫
        " 2d   "   II   "   ⎬ GOOD
        " 6th   " IV II or VI   " ⎭
        " 3d less good because of the harmony!
        " 7th merely substitution

before 2   4. because IV or II degree ⎫
        "   6.   "   IV II VI   "   ⎬ GOOD
        "   3. because melodic *scale*[131] ⎭
        "   5. because mere substitution
        "   7.   "   "   "

before 7, the 2d   because   II. degree ⎫
               4th   "   II.IV.II. (tritone) ⎬ GOOD
               6th because part of the scale ⎭

not very good :
the 3d not impossible because the component 3d is 7 of III.[36]
the 5th merely substitution

What is merely substitution is not outright bad, but to {be used} only for rhythmic reasons

????

---

35. Compare the following list with ibid., 38–52.

36. I.e., the third of VII is the seventh of III.

50 *Zusammenhang*

Skalateile die in den 1. Ton münden{,} wirken immer als Kadenz, weil die Tonleiter ja nur die Tonart ausdrückt.

{1:28}   Weitere Kadenzen

4) 451	7) 421	10) 271	13/14) 351!, 751	19) 151	20) 121
5) 251	8) 621	11) 471!!	15/16) 521, 721	21) 171	
6) 651	9) 321	12) 671	17/18) 371, 571		

Tritonus

Was kann vor 4 kommen? der 6. 3. 5. 1. 2 (7!!)
" 2 " ? " 4. 3. 1. 5. 6 (7.)
" 6 " ? " 3. 4. 2. 5. 7. 1
" 7 " ? " 6. 2. 4!! 5. 3. 1
" 3 " ? " 4. 2. 5 6 7 1
" 1 " ? " 2 3 4 5 6 7
" 5 " ? " 1 2 3 4 6 7

Ausführung auf dem Nebenblatt
Besprechung des Ungeeingneten etc.

— o —

Die Tonart wird nach derselben Methode *verlassen*, wie im harmonischen Satz; ebenso festgehalten, u. befestigt. Nur treten an Stelle der Harmonien die Töne und Tonfolgen. Ist es dort darauf angekommen, entsprechende Akkorde und Akkordfolgen zu finden, so handelt es sich hier um Töne und Tonfolgen. Nach dem über das Ausdrücken Gesagten{,} kann das nicht mehr schwierig sein und es genügt wohl einige Beispiele anzuführen und zu besprechen.

51 Coherence

Parts of the scale that end on the 1st tone always have the effect of a cadence because the scale expresses only the key.

{1:28}[37]   Additional cadences

4) 4 5 1	7) 4 2 1	10) 2 7 1	13/14) 3 5 1!, 7 5 1	19) 1 5 1	20) 1 7 1
5) 2 5 1	8) 6 2 1	11) 4 7 1!!	15/16) 5 2 1, 7 2 1	21) 1 2 1	
6) 6 5 1	9) 3 2 1	12) 6 7 1	17/18) 3 7 1, 5 7 1		

			tritone
What can occur before	4?	the 6th, 3d, 5th, 1st, 2d (7!!)
"	"	2?	the 4th, 3d, 1st, 5th, 6th, (7th)
"	"	6?	the 3d, 4th, 2d, 5th, 7th, 1st
"	"	7?	the 6th, 2d, 4th!! , 5th, 3d, 1st
"	"	3?	the 4th, 2d, 5th, 6th, 7th, 1st
"	"	1?	the 2d, 3d, 4th, 5th, 6th, 7th
"	"	5?	the 1st, 2d, 3d, 4th, 6th, 7th

Illustration on the accompanying sheet[38]
Discussion of what is unsuitable, etc.

— o —

The key is *abandoned* or, on the other hand, established and strengthened by the same method as in a harmonic sentence, except that tones and their successions appear in place of harmonies. If the issue in the first case is to find suitable chords and successions of chords, the concern here is with tones and their successions. After what has been said about the means of expression, this can no longer be difficult, and it probably is sufficient to cite and discuss several examples.

---

37. In the original manuscript this is an insertion.

38. See example below.

52 Zusammenhang

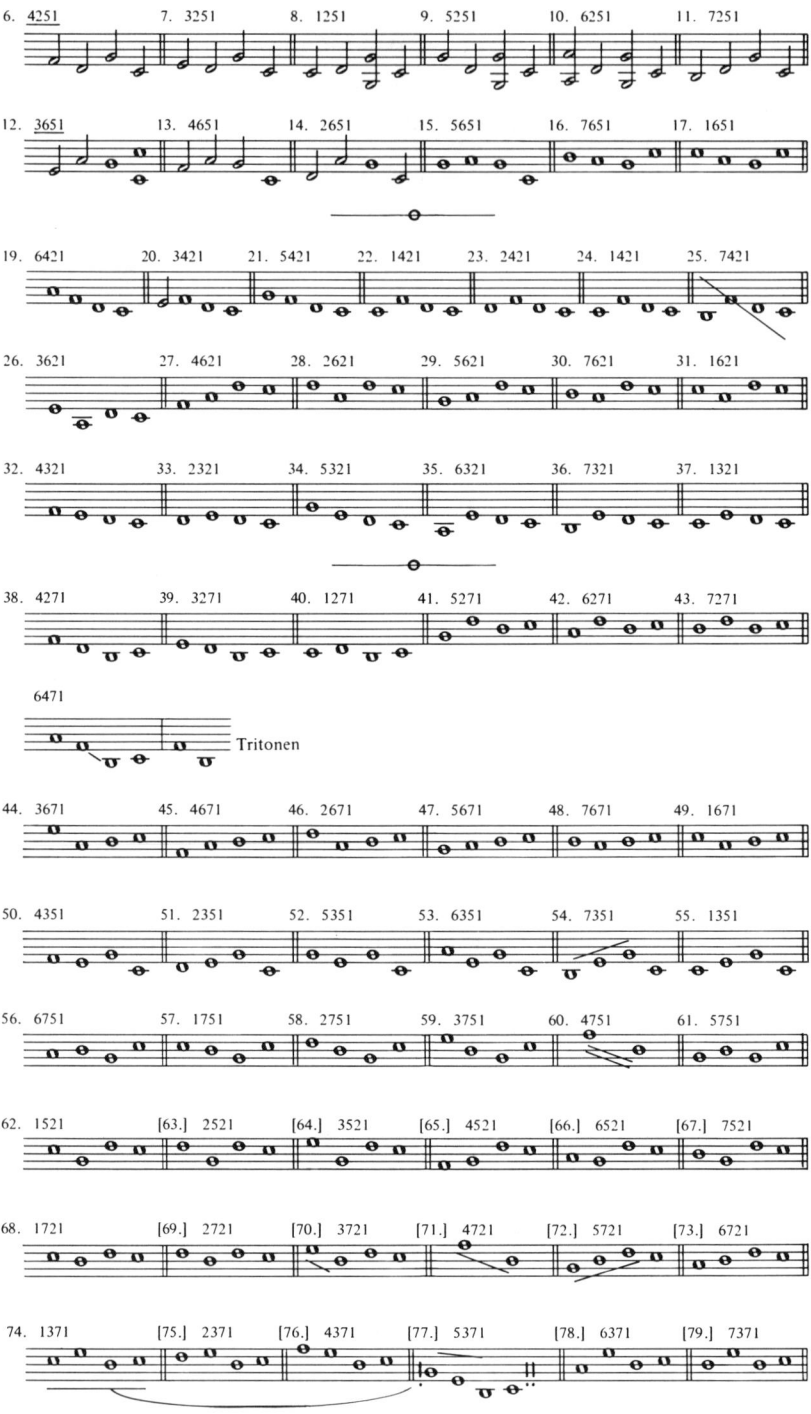

Coherence

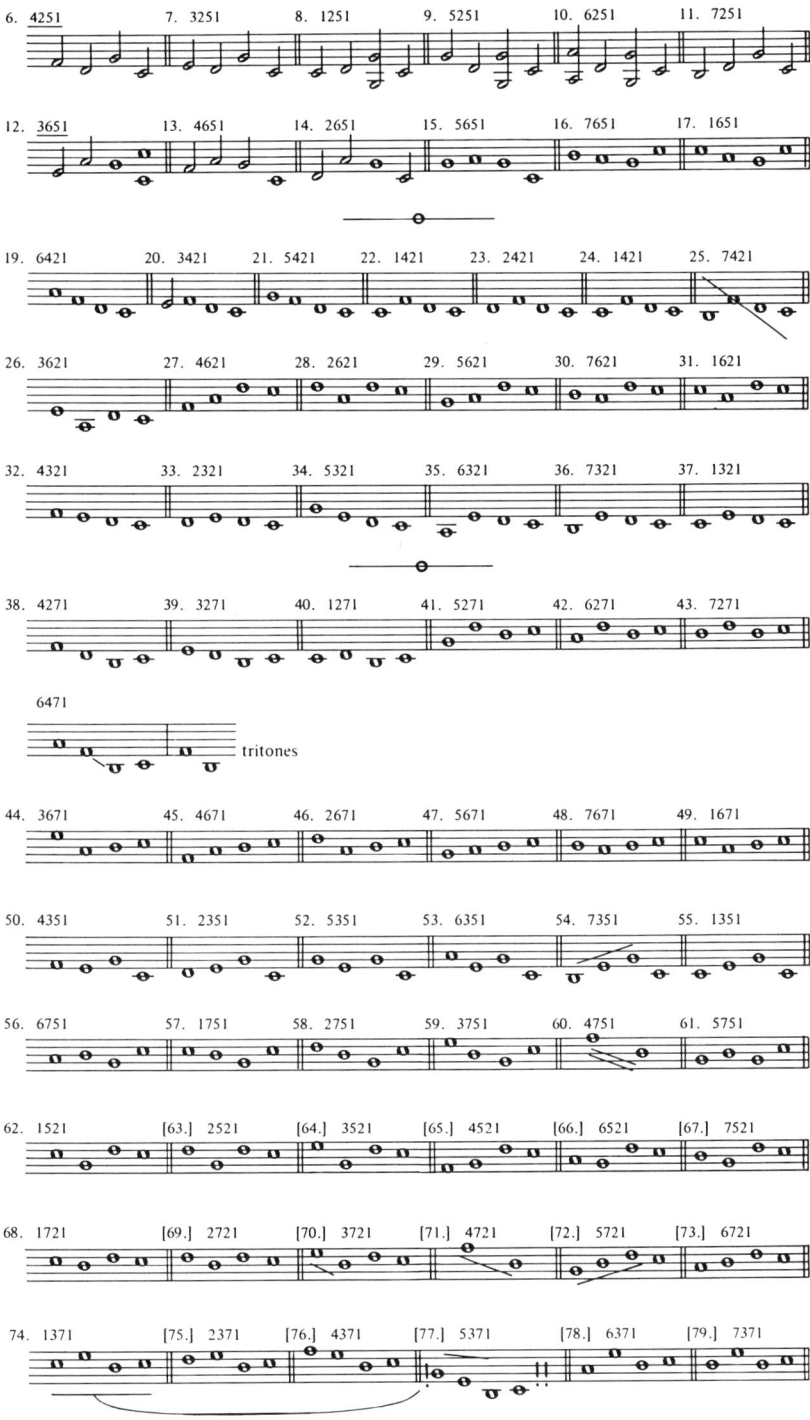

54 *Zusammenhang*

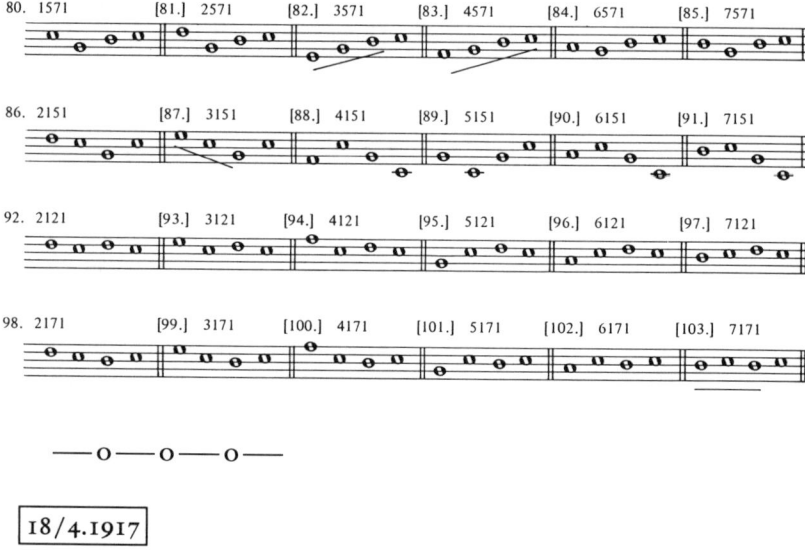

─── o ── o ── o ───

18/4.1917

Inwiefern sind a) *Takt*   — a) *zusammenhalten{d}*
              b) *Rhyt{h}mus* — b) *auseinandertreibend?*

Die Einheitlichkeit des Taktes ist insofern ein zusammenhaltendes Formprinzip, als durch den Takt das Stück eine gewisse Charakteristik bekommt. Da jede Tonfolge in bestimmten Zeiträumen auf unbetonte oder betonte {Taktteile}

{1:29}

trifft, und umgekehrt die betonten und unbetonten Taktteile in jede Tonfolge auf bestimmte Art Unterschied hineinbringen, wird dieselbe Tonfolge in verschieden{en} Taktarten verschieden wirken.

Ebenso verhält es sich mit dem Rhyt{h}mus

Noch deutlicher wird dieser Umstand, wenn der Rhyt{h}mus aus langen und kurzen Noten besteht. Bsp: Dieselbe Tonfolge in verschiedene Takten

in anderer Betonung

55 Coherence

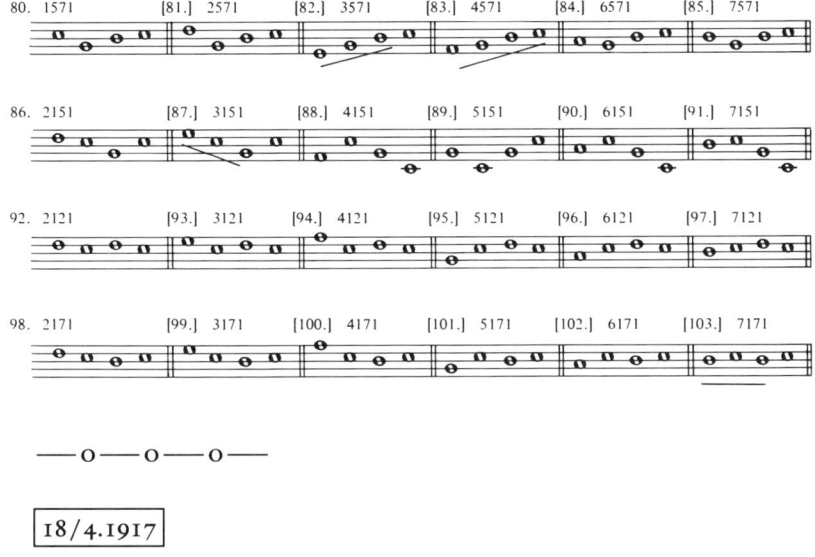

— o — o — o —

18/4.1917

To what extent are   a) meter } — a) binding
                                b) rhythm } — b) separating?

Uniformity of meter is a binding principle of form insofar as the piece acquires a certain characteristic through its meter. Since each succession of tones within particular time spans falls on stressed and unstressed

{1:29}

beats and, conversely, stressed and unstressed beats introduce a certain differentiation into each succession of tones, the same succession will operate differently in different kinds of meter.

The same applies to rhythm.

This circumstance becomes even clearer if the rhythm consists of long and short notes. Ex.: The same succession of tones in different meters

with other stress

56 Zusammenhang

dieselbe Tonfolge in verschi*e*ndenen Rhyt[h]men und Taktarten

Diese Charakteristik ist desto ausgesprochener je länger sie dauert und je öfter sich gewisse Ereignisse wiederholen (Rhyt[h]men) zBsp

XXXX zeigt wie selbst sehr ähnliche Formen sich dennoch unterscheiden

{1:30}

Die Charakteristik wird weiter erhöht, wenn die Wiederholungen motivartig erfolgen weiter,[9] wenn Variation und Kontrast dazu tritt.

---

9. weiter erfolgen.

57 Coherence

{1:30}

Such characteristics are further heightened if the repetitions occur in a motivic manner, {and} if variation
and contrast additionally appear.

58 *Zusammenhang*

Wie stark die zusammenfassende Kraft des Taktes ist{,} erkennt man an dem Kontrast den zwei aufeinanderfolgende Stücke verschiedenen Taktes bewirken. Oder schon, wenn in einem kurzen Satz ein Taktwechsel eintritt, z.Bsp.

Dieses Sätzchen fällt für unser Formgefühl bloss deswegen nicht auseinander{,} weil wir 1. aus der modernen Musik{,} die sich vielfach in Prosa oder rhyt{h}misierter Prosa ausdrück{t} an komplicierteres gewöhnt sind und 2. sogar die *verhältnismässige* Regelmässigkeit mit der $\frac{3}{4}$ und $\frac{4}{4}$ hier wechseln{,} bereits als Wiederholung, ja als Regelmässigkeit empfunden wird, wobei nicht einmal die tatsächliche Unregelmässigkeit Regelmässigkeit empfunden wird, wobei nicht einmal die tatsächliche Unregelmässigkeit stört. 3. Weil dieses Sätzchen durch eine andere Eigentümlichkeit geschlossen wirkt: die

{1:32}

durch Klammern bezeichneten Absätze 1 2 3 4 sind nichts anderes als beinahe genaue Wiederholungen der 1. Tonfolge von anderen Tönen aus.

— o —

{1:33}

22/4.1917   Der *2-taktige* Rhyt{h}mus (Ursprungsrhy{t}hmus) kommt von unseren 2 Beinen (Händen) und von unserem Schritt.

— o —

der 3-taktige [] könnte vom Schrittwechsel kommen. Andere Rhyt{h}men entstehen, wenn ein Holzschlegel auf einer gespannten Haut selbsttätig vibriert.

— o —

59 Coherence

The strength of the meter's binding power can be seen from the contrast between two successive pieces of different meter. Or even if a change of meter occurs within a short excerpt, for ex.

This short phrase does not violate our feeling for form, and does not fall apart, because 1. we are accustomed through modern music to more complicated material that is frequently expressed in prose or rhythmicized prose, and 2. even the *comparative regularity* with which $\frac{3}{4}$ and $\frac{4}{4}$ alternate is already perceived here as repetition, even as regularity, and even the actual irregularity is not considered disturbing. 3. Because this short phrase gives the impression of completeness, due to another characteristic: the

{I:32}[39]

phrases 1 2 3 4, designated by brackets, are nothing other than almost exact repetitions of the 1st tone sequence starting from different tones.

— o —

{I:33}

22/4.1917   *2-beat* rhythm (original rhythm) comes from our two legs (hands) and from our gait.

— o —

The 3-beat rhythm [♩. ♪ ♩ (♩. ♫ ♩)] could come from a change of step. Other rhythms arise when a mallet spontaneously vibrates on a taut hide.

— o —

---

39. Schoenberg skips a page here.

Die Umkehrung
u." Symetrie } entsteht aus dem Spiegelbild

— o —

Wir ahmen bewusst und unbewusst in Tönen nach, was wir in anderen Materialien auch mit anderen Sinnen wahrgenommen haben. Auch übertragen wir unsere Denkweise (jeder Art) auf das Material der Musik.

— o —

{1:33} 23/4.1917 Der *künstlerisch verwertbare* Zusammenhang muss für die zusammenhängen den Teile *charakteristisch* sein, die zusammenhängenden Beziehungen dürfen dem Wesen der Teile nicht ganz fremd und die Verbinung etwa nur äusserlich sein.

In diesem Sinne wird man gewiss nicht von einem künstlerischen Zusammenhang reden können, wenn Teile in der Weise verbunden sind, wie etwa in dem folgenden Fall:

An ein Stück Kork ist mit Kleister ein Papierstreifen geklebt, an diesen eine Hühnerfeder, an diese mit Schnur ein Nagel angebunden.

Gewiss hängen solche Dinge zusammen. Aber es fehlt dem Ganzen jede charakteristische Beziehung. Auch eine Leine ist nur an eine Stange gebunden und kann eine Angel bilden. Hier ist es der *Sinn, der Zweck*, der die Verbindung dieser Gegenstände legitimiert. Aber auch nur dieser. Denn ohne einen solchen, besitzen

dürfte für die musikalischen Fragen nicht in Betracht {kommen}

{1:34} Dinge keinen Zusammenhang

Welches sind bei der Angel die verbindenden Zusammenhänge (Wiederholungen etc.)?

Im Gebiet des Materiellen scheint oft an Stelle der gemeinsamen Theile der Berührungspunkt zu treten, der gemeinsam ist.

Es ist nötig, dass ich mich aufs Musikalische beschränke

— o —

23/4.1917
Musikalische Gedanken können zusammenhängen

Inversion and symmetry } arise from the mirror form.

— o —

We consciously and unconsciously imitate in tones what we have perceived, even with different senses, in other materials. We also apply our way of thinking (of every kind) to the material of music.

— o —

|23/4.1917| *Artistically usable* coherence must {bear the} *characteristics* of the related parts; the connecting relationships should not be entirely foreign to the nature of the parts nor should the connection {between parts and connectives} be merely superficial.

In this sense, it is certainly impossible to speak of an artistic coherence if, for example, parts are connected as in the following case:

A strip of paper is glued to a piece of cork; a chicken feather is glued to this, to which a nail is tied with string.

Such things are certainly connected. But the whole is lacking any characteristic relationship. Likewise a line merely tied to a stick can form a fishing rod. Here it is the *sense, the purpose*, that legitimizes the connection of these objects — but only this purpose. Because without such a purpose,

{*This*} *is unsuitable for musical questions.*[40]

things have no coherence.

What are the coherences in the fishing rod (repetitions, etc.)?

In the realm of material objects, the point of contact often takes the place of parts held in common.

It is necessary that I confine myself to the musical.

— o —

23/4.1917
Musical ideas can cohere

---

40. Inserted in margin.

musikalischer Inhalt	1. durch die Tonfolgen (Intervalle, Rhyt{h}men{,} Phrasen)
2. durch den Rhyt{h}mus
3. durch die Harmonie
4. durch Zugehörigkeit
(a) zu einer gemeinsamen Harmonie oder
(b) einer gemeinsamen Stimme
5. durch Ähnlichkeit oder Gleichheit der Gliederung
5b. dadurch, dass beide einem dritten Gedanken verwandt sind
durch den sonstigen seelischen Inhalt, da Musik aus Gefühlsanlässen geschrieben wird, auf die Gefühle wirkt	6. durch den Ausdruck
7.   " die Stimmung
8.   " den Charakter
9. durch den Text im Lied
10.   "   "   " im Recitativ
11.   "   "   " in symphonischen Dichtungen
12.   "   "   " in der Oper
13.   " die Scene "   "   "
14.   " Bilder die bewusst äussere Verbindung sind
15. durch   "   " unbewusst   "   " sind

— o —

durch ein Formales	16. scheinbar zufällige Berührungspunkte
etc

%

{1:35} Alle diese auf Seite 34 genannten Zusammenhänge können auftreten
    als Wiederholung
     " Gegensatz
     " Variation
     " Entwicklung

Coherence

musical content
- 1. through the successions of tones (intervals, rhythms, phrases)
- 2. through rhythm
- 3. through harmony
- 4. through belonging (a) to a common harmony or (b) to a common voice
- 5. through similarity or identity of articulation.
- 5b. in that both are related to a third idea

through the other types of spiritual content, as music is composed from the promptings of states of mind that are affected by feelings
- 6. through expression
- 7. through mood
- 8. through character
- 9. through the text in a song
- 10. through the text in a recitative
- 11. through the text in symphonic poems
- 12. through the text in opera
- 13. through the scene in opera
- 14. through images that are a conscious, external connection
- 15. through images that are an unconscious, external connection

— o —

through something formal
- 16. seemingly random points of contact
- etc.

%

{1:35} All these coherences mentioned on page 34 can occur
    as repetition
    as contrast
    as variation
    as development

— o —

Der Zusammenhang kann
   1. unterstrichen werden
   2. verschleiert   "
   3. verborgen   "
   4. kann er auch anfangs vollkommen unsichtbar sein und erst nach und nach *enthüllt werden*

— o —

Er kann   1) direkt und unmittelbar sein
            2) indirekt oder mittelbar

{Kontrapunkt}

{1:2}   Zshg

11.IV.1917

Im Gegensatz zu den sogenannten *Ripien- oder Füllstimmen*, welche bloss die zur Vollständigkeit der Harmonie nötige Bewegung ausführen, spricht man von *selbstständigen* Stimmen.

Was ist eine selbstständige Stimme?

LsnDef

Eine *selbstständige Stimme* ist jene, die in Form, Ausdruck und Entwicklung unabhängig ist von irgendwelchen anderen, etwa mit ihr gleichzeitig erklingenden Stimmen.

Mit diesen hängt sie bloss insoferne zusammen (und von ihnen bloss insoweit ab) als es die Erfordernisse des (harmonischen) Zusammenklangs und der deutlichen Abhebung bedingen.

— o —

Coherence can
- 1. be underlined
- 2. be veiled
- 3. be hidden
- 4. it can also be completely invisible at the beginning and only gradually *be revealed*

— o —

It can
- 1) be direct and immediate
- 2) indirect or mediating

{Counterpoint}

{1:2}   Coh. [41]

11.IV.1917

In contrast to the so-called *Ripieno or filler voices*, which merely carry out the movement necessary to complete the harmony, one speaks of *independent* voices.[42]

What is an independent voice?

Precepts and definitions

An *independent voice* is one which in form, expression, and development is independent of any other voices that may be sounding simultaneously with it.

It is connected with (and dependent on) these {voices} merely insofar as the requirements of (harmonic) sound combination and clear profiling demand.

---

41. In Schoenberg's index this section of material is listed as appropriate for both "Zusammenhang" and "Kontrapunkt": hence the designation "Coh." (Coherence) at the top of the page.

42. For further discussion of independent and dependent voices, see Schoenberg, "Der musikalische Gedanke und die Logik, Technik und Kunst seiner Darstellung," 85–86.

66 *Kontrapunkt*

—o—

Worin besteht die Unabhängigkeit einer Stimme (Ist die 2te Stimme im Kanon unabhängig?)

Die <u>Unabhängigkeit der Entwicklung</u> einer Stimme besteht darin, dass sie lediglich den *Bedürfnissen* und *Möglichkeiten* ihres Motives folgt.

(Das ist auch bei der 2.Stimme des Kanon, und bei jeder Imitation der Fall. Eine unselbstständige Stimme wäre nicht in der Lage das Motiv so fortzusetzen, wie

{1:3}

es die zweite Stimme des Kanons tut, sondern {sie} hätte nur die Aufgabe und das Bestreben die Harmonie vollständig zu machen).

Aber es kommen auch in rein harmonischen Sätzen, Stimmen, oder in diesen mehr oder weniger lange Stellen vor, die *melodisch* sind, den Eindruck von Selbstständigkeit machen und sogar hie und da nach einem Motiv aussehen.

Was ist melodische Stimmführung?

In der Regel begnügen sich rein-harmonische Sätze mit der *Vermeidung des Unmelodischen* (negative Erklärungsmethode) welches darin besteht, dass an Stelle gewisser schwer <u>*fasslicher Intervalle*</u>* und <u>*Rhyt{h}-men*</u> nur solche gesetz werden, deren Gebrauch durch die Konvention geheiligt ist.

*ZBSp

Es ist falsch schon[10] eine solche Stimme melodisch zu nennen. Sie ist bloss: nicht unmelodisch.

Aber es giebt Zwischenformen, die dadurch fast melodisch erscheinen, dass sich einzelne Teile wiederholen (ermöglicht durch Zufällig-

---

10. Es ist schon falsch.

67 Counterpoint

— o —

Of what does the independence of a voice consist? (Is the 2d voice in a canon independent?) ↑

The *independence of development* in a voice merely consists of following the *requirements* and *possibilities* of its motive.

{1:3}

(This is also the case with the 2d voice of a canon and with every imitation. A dependent voice would not be able to continue the motive the way the second voice of a canon does; rather, it would have only the task and aim of completing the harmony).

However, *melodic* voices occur in purely harmonic phrases, voices, or within more or less long {harmonic} passages.[43] {Such voices} give the impression of independence and occasionally even look like a motive.

What is melodic voice-leading?

As a rule, purely harmonic phrases manage by *avoiding the unmelodic* (negative method of explanation), which means that in place of *certain intervals**[44] *and rhythms* which are difficult to comprehend, only those are resorted to whose use is sanctioned by convention.

It is quite wrong to call such a voice melodic. It is merely not unmelodic.

*For example

However, there are intermediate forms that seem almost melodic in that individual parts are repeated (this is made possible by chance occurrences, even exploited ones, by repetitions in the main voice, etc.).

---

43. For example, a polyphonic passage within a basically homophonic work.

44. The example in the manuscript is placed parenthetically at the bottom of the page; hence the asterisk.

keiten, auch ausgenützte, durch Wiederholungen in der Haupstimme etc) und in manchen Fällen kann eine solche Füllstimme bis zu einem gewissen Grad an primitiv organisierte Melodien erinnern, umsomehr, als eben solche Melodien selbst nicht viel höher stehen als Füllstimmen.

Aber von *melodischer* Stimm-

%

{1:4} führung kann man mit Recht nicht sprechen, wenn für die *Fasslichkeit* etwas mehr geschieht als die Vermeidung des Unfasslichen.

Eine *melodisch Stimme* ist demnach jene, deren Form und Bau so ist, dass ihr *musikalischer Inhalt musikalisch fasslich ist.*

—— o ——

{1:16} 14/IV.1917

Bedingungen für die 1. Aufgabe im Kontrapunkt:
ein selbständiges, einstimmiges Sätzchen von 3–9 Takten
1) *Warum 3–9 Takte?*
weil die Tonleiter 7 Töne hat und somit bereits 2 mal Wiederholungen eintreten müssen (Monotonie)
2) *Was ist ein Sätzchen?*
Eine durch Anfang und Ende in sich abgeschlossen Tonfolge. Anfang und Ende: Bestimmung der Tonart.

—— o ——

{1:32} 20/4.1917   Im Kontrapunktbuch (und wo nötig auch in den anderen) kann immer bei solchen Angelegenheiten, die bereits in meiner *Harmonielehre* stehen, auf die betreffende Quelle verwiesen und bloss kurz der Haupt-Inhalt angegeben werden.

—— o ——

20/4.1917   1. Aufgabe *im Kontrapunkt* CF in ₀ selbst erfinden

And in some case, such a filler voice can to a certain extent recall primitively organized melodies, all the more so since such melodies themselves are not much more advanced than filler voices.⁴⁵

But one cannot properly speak of *melodic* voice-leading

%

{1:4} if something more happens for the sake of *comprehensibility* than merely the avoidance of incomprehensibility.

Accordingly, a *melodic voice* is one whose form and structure is such that its *musical content is musically comprehensible.*

— o —

{1:16} 14/IV.1917

Conditions for the 1st exercise in counterpoint:
a short independent one-voice phrase of 3–9 measures
1) *Why 3–9 measures?*
because the scale has 7 tones and consequently repetitions must occur twice (monotony)
2) *What is a small phrase?*
A succession of tones complete in itself through a beginning and an end. Beginning and end: determination of the tonality.

— o —

{1:32} 20/4.1917   With such matters as are already contained in my *Theory of Harmony*, the relevant source can always be pointed out and the main content merely stated briefly in the book on counterpoint (and wherever necessary, in the others as well).

— o —

20/4.1917   1. exercise *in counterpoint* to invent a CF in whole notes

---

45. For definitions of melody, see Schoenberg, "Der musikalische Gedanke und die Logik, Technik und Kunst seiner Darstellung," 37–38, 103–4; idem, *Fundamentals*, 102.

70 *Kontrapunkt*

II. CF in ♩ (Betonung berücksichtigen) Welche Gesetze?

III. zu selbsterfundenem (und gegebenem) CF eine 2te Stimme (strenger Satz)

IV. die III. in ♩

V. CF in ♩ Ktrp in 𝅝

VI. CF in ♩ Stimmen in ♩
        usw eventuell 3te Stimme dazu

x^te Aufgabe 2 Selbstständige Stimmen gleichzeitig erfinden.

— o —

{Notenbeispiele zu Kontrapunkt, Formenlehre Instrumentation u. Zusammenhang}

{1}

? * = illegible

71 *Counterpoint*

      II. CF in half notes (take the accent into consideration) Which laws?

     III. to set a second voice (strict composition) to a self-invented (and given) CF

    IV. the III.[46] in half notes

     V. CF in half notes, counterpoint in whole notes

   VI. CF in half notes, voices in half notes, etc., possibly a third voice in addition

x[th] exercise to invent two independent voices simultaneously.

— o —

{Examples for Counterpoint, Instruction in Form, Instrumentation, and Coherence}

{1}

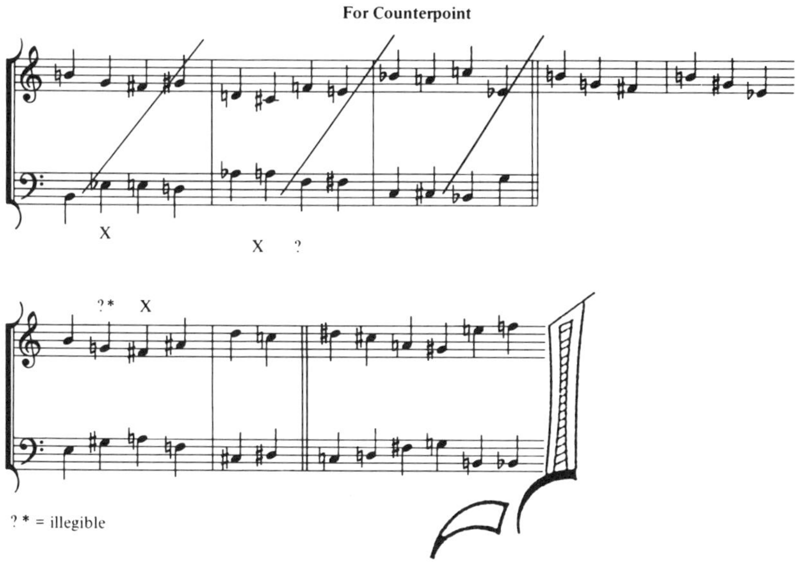

*? * = illegible*

---

46. I.e., the requirements in III above.

72 *Kontrapunkt*

{3}

73 *Counterpoint*

{3}[47]

---

47. Page 2 is blank.

74 *Kontrapunkt*

{4}

{5}

75 *Counterpoint*

{4}[48]

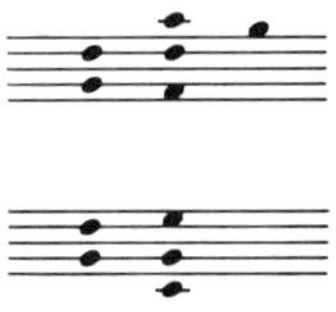

{5}[49]

---

48. P.3 verso.

49. Pp.7–19 following this example are blank.

{6}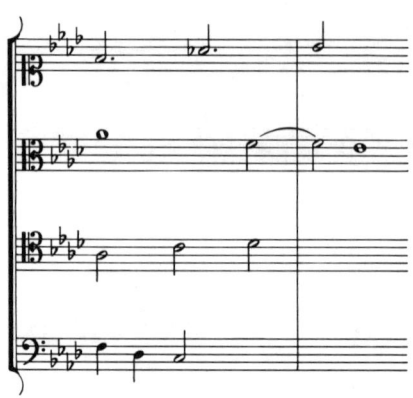

{Instrumentation}

{BOOK OUTLINE}

{II:14} 21/4.1917

Entwurf zu einer Disposition der *Instr.Lehre*

77 *Instrumentation*

{6}

{Instrumentation}

{BOOK OUTLINE}

{II:14}   21/4.1917

Sketch for an arrangement of the *Instruction in Instrumentation*[50]

---

50. The late writings on orchestration (see Christensen and Christensen, *Literary Legacy*, 101–6) have little to do with this early text because of technological advances. Schoenberg later intended that a student learn orchestration by notating orchestral combinations from a phonograph record:

> A master hears the sound of the full orchestra and possesses the capacity, the knowledge and the experience to analyse his idea and to find out what composes this special sound.... A beginner in orchestration might not be capable of hearing in his imagination distinctly a sonority—the record replaces the imagined sound, by a material one.... Extracts of orchestral compositions (of which records, and if possible—also scores are available, in schools at least, or in libraries) shall be made in form of particells, in two to six (or more) staves. They must contain everything, every voice, every accompanying figure or harmony which is to be found in the full orchestra score. But there must not appear any indication of the manner in which it is orchestrated.... These particells should be used as follows: The student has to receive a record of the section. He may play it as often as he wants, also partly only. While he listens, he reads the particell and tries to hear every voice, and to find out who plays it. When he starts writing in the score, he need not try to give exactly the same sonority as that which he hears, but a similar one.
>
> The teacher *alone* has the score and will discuss the difference between the masterwork and the student's attempt. (From "Materials for Orchestration," catalogued as 1-1.1 in Christensen and Christensen, *Literary Legacy*, 101.)

Setzkunst

Einleitung: I. Bisherige Lehrmethode 1) ist eigentlich bloss a) Instrumentarkunde b) einige ungenügende Versuche, Regeln für einzelne Zusammenstellungen zu geben, c) einige Anweisungen die lediglich vom Geschmack ausgehen, d) " " " praktischen Erfahrungen entsprechen, e) einiges über Ausdruck, Stimmung Charakter.

2) es fehlt dagegen a) eine genaue Beschreibung des „*Volums*," Vergleiche der Tonstärken und Farben und Detail durchgeführt, b) Anleitungen zur Wahl der Besetzungen, ... Berücksichtigung der Wirkung der Stricharten etc.

3) Hauptsächlich ist die alte Lehre: *Instrumentenkunde* und nimmt an, dass alles Uebrige durchs Gehör und Talent gefunden werde

II. Hauptfehler der alten Methode: *die wahre Grundlage für alle Instrumentation ist der Satz*. Vorerst muss also der Schüler wählen: wie soll ein Satz beschaffen sein, der für diese oder jene Instrumentenzusammenstellung geeignet ist. Ferner daher ist die wichtigste Forderung: *für's Orchester erfinden*

       1. Theil

I. Kapitel *Satzkunst*

Welche Arten von Satz giebt es?

1. stilistisch: a) Homophonen
     b) Mischform{en}   } mit allen Unterabteilungen
     c) Polyphone

2. hinsichtlich der Lagenverhältnisse der Stimmen (Lage des Themas oben, unten, etc.)

3. hinnsichtlich des Verhältnisses zwischen Haupt- u. Nebenstimmen

4. hinsichtlich der Lage und Bedeutung der Harmonie

5. hinsichtlich der Bewegung (Tempo, etc.)

6. " der Deutlichkeit

7. " der Stricharten, Phrasierungen, Betonungen, etc.

8. hinsichtlich des Ausdrucks u. Charakters und der Charakteristik

II. Instrumentenkunde

Setting for Orchestra

Introduction: I. The teaching method up to the present 1) is actually nothing more than a) information about instruments b) some inadequate attempts at providing rules for individual combinations, c) some instructions based merely on taste, d) some instructions in keeping with practical experience, e) several comments about expression, mood, character.

2) There is lacking, on the other hand, a) a precise description of the *scope*, thoroughgoing comparisons of volumes and colors and detail, b) methodical instructions for the choice of instrumentation, consideration of the effect of types of bowing, etc.

3) Essentially the old method is: *instrumentation*, and {it} assumes that everything else will be found out by means of the ear and through talent.

II. The main defect of the old method: *the true basis for all instrumentation is composition itself.* Therefore the student must first choose: what is the nature of a composition, so that may be suitable for this or that instrumental combination. Hence the most important requirement is *to invent for the orchestra*

1st Part

I. Chapter on *composition*
    What kinds of composition are there?
    1. stylistically: a) homophonic
                     b) mixed forms   } with all subdivisions
                     c) polyphonic
    2. with regard to the registers of the voices (position of the theme above, below, etc.)
    3. with regard to the relationship between main and subordinate voices
    4. with regard to the arrangement and significance of the harmony
    5. with regard to the motion (tempo, etc.)
    6. with regard to clarity
    7. with regard to the kinds of bowing, phrasing, emphasis, etc.
    8. with regard to expression and character and of particular characteristics

II. Instrumentation

80 *Instrumentation*

      III. Welche Bedingungen stellen die Instrumente an den Satz?

      IV. Inwiefern sind die Instrumente geeignet, die Bedingungen des Satzes zu erfüllen?

      V. Vom Klang

Welche Arten des Klangs ausser gut schön etc.

Mischklang Soloklang etc.

{II:16}   VI. Welche Bedingungen stellt der Klang an den Satz?

Siehe III. VII. Welche Bedingungen stellen die Instrumente an den (Satz) Klang

      ?VIII. "   "   stellt der Klang an die Instrumente? Siehe VI

II. Theil
Setzkunst

I. Allgemeine Darstellung

    a) der *gebräuchlichen* ⎫ Kammermusik, Orchester, Chor,
                                 ⎬ Lied, Duette etc. und *Gesang*
    b) einiger möglichen ⎭ *Instrumentenzusammenstellungen*

II. Gründe und Erwägungen für die *Wahl der Besetzung*

    1) *Stilfragen* die für die obigen Erwägungen massgebend sind

    2) Woran erkennt man die Eignung eines Satzes für eine bestimmte Besetzung

    3) *Aphoristisch:* einige praktische Beispiele falscher Einsicht

    4) Einfluss des *Charakters und Ausdrucks* auf die Wahl der Besetzung

    5) Besprechung an Hand von Beispielen über die Vorzüge, Eigenthümlichkeiten und Mängel mancher Besetzung.

    6) Welchen Forderungen wird eine Besetzung immer entsprechen müssen

81 *Instrumentation*

  III. What conditions do the instruments impose on composition?

  IV. To what extent are the instruments suited to fulfill the conditions of composition?⁵¹

  V. Concerning the sound

Which kinds of sound in addition to good, beautiful, etc. Mixture of sound, solo sound, etc.⁵²

{II:16} VI. What conditions does sonority impose on compositions?

See III. VII. What conditions do the instruments impose on the sonority of the (setting)?

  ? VIII. " " does sonority impose on the instruments? See VI.

2d Part
Scoring Technique

I. General representation
  a) of the *customary* ⎫ chamber music, orchestra, chorus,
         ⎬ song, duet, etc. and *singing*
  b) of several possible ⎭ *instrumental combinations*

II.⁵³: Reasons and considerations for the *choice of the instrumentation*

  1) *Questions of style* that are decisive for the above considerations

  2) How does one recognize the suitability of a composition for a particular instrumentation?

  3) *Aphoristic:* several practical examples of erroneous insight

  4) Influence of *character and expression* on the choice of the instrumentation

  5) Discussion, on the basis of examples, about the merits, peculiarities, and deficiencies of some instrumentations.

  6) Which demands will a particular instrumentation always have to comply with

---

51. "Setting" is also a possible translation of *Satzes*.

52. In margin.

53. Schoenberg first numbered item II as item I and items 1–6 as items 2–7, apparently as subheadings of item I. Subsequently he assigned the roman numerals II–VII to items II and 1–5, before arriving at the numbering reproduced here. A brace spanning the present items 1–4 directs an illegible marginal note that apparently concerned this reorganization.

82 *Instrumentation*

    a) für mindestens den Höhen und Tiefen-Umfang der Komposition geeignete Instrumente
    b) womöglich einen kleinen Ueberschuss davon.
    c) Instrumente von genügender Stärke oder Zartheit
    d) entsprechende Beweglichkeit oder Schwere
    e) Meistens wird es nötig sein, eine Gruppe oder ein Instrument zu haben, das imstande ist, im grössten *ff* dominierend das Thema zu bringen.
7) Inwiefern können die Instrumente diesen

%

{II:18}

III. *Umgekehrt:* wenn man aus irgendwelchen praktischen Gründen (zBsp. materielle; oder man hat den 1. Akt einer Oper oder Symphonie für diese Besetzung komponiert etc) an eine bestimmte Besetzung gebunden ist, welche Erwägungen sind dann massgebend{?}

1) Ökonomische Ausnützung der Mittel; Berücksichtigung der Höhepunkte; Achtung auf Mannigfaltigkeit; Charakteristik.

2) Inwiefern kann die Wirkung eines Instrumentes durch andere erzielt oder ersetzt werden.

3) die Frage der dominierenden Gruppe

III. Theil (praktisch)

1. Der Satz für die verschiedenen Instrumente
    1) einzeln
    2) in Gruppen zu 2, 3, 4, 5, etc Solistisch (Kammer Musik)
    3) im Orchester
        a) Streichorchester
        b) kleines (Varieté-)Orchester
        c) kleines klassisches Symphonie-Orchester

{II:19}

        d) das grosse klassische Symphonie Orchester
        e)   ″ kleine moderne   ″   ″
        f) das grosse   ″   ″   ″
        g) einige besonders grosse Orchester
        h) Gesang und Orchester
        i) Chor   ″   ″

a) for at least the registral span of the instruments suited for the composition
b) if possible, a slight excess of that
c) instruments of sufficient strength or delicacy
d) suitable flexibility or weightiness
e) usually it will be necessary to have one group {of instruments} or one instrument that in passages of maximal *ff* is capable of bringing the theme into dominance.

7) To what extent the instruments are capable {of this}[54]

%

{II:18} III. *Conversely:* if one is committed to a particular instrumentation for some practical reasons (for example, for material reasons or because one has composed the first act of an opera or symphony for this instrumentation, etc.), which considerations are then decisive?

1) economical exploitation of the means; considerations of the climaxes; attention to variety; {observance of} characteristics.

2) to the extent that the effect of an instrument may be achieved or replaced by others

3) the question of the dominating group

3d Part (practical)

I. Composition for the various instruments
  1) singly
  2) in groups of 2, 3, 4, 5, etc., soloistic (chamber music)
  3) in the orchestra
      a) string orchestra
      b) small (theater) orchestra
      c) small classical symphony orchestra
{II:19} d) the large classical symphony orchestra
      e) " small modern   "   "
      f) the large   "   "   "
      g) some especially large orchestras
      h) voice and orchestra
      i) chorus   "   "

---

54. The remainder of this sentence is omitted.

84 *Instrumentation*

        k) Solo Instrument mit Orchester
        l) das Solo im Orchester
        m) das Opern Orchester

—— o ——

Aphoristisch: Merkwürdige Phänomene
    Sind Oktaven stärker als Einklang? Werden starke Instrumente stärker durch Verdopplung?   "   "   "
    Zusetzung anderer?
    Das Solo-Instr. im Orchester.
    Die Nachbarschaft.
    Ueber Deutlichkeit (Was ist sie? Ihr Zweck? Ihre Berechtigung? Ihre technischen Bedingungen.) Die Wirkung bequemer und unbequemer Lagen. Homogene u. Heterogene Mischungen.

{II:20}   Ueber dünne u. dicke Instrumentation. Geräuschstimmen etc.

{ON THE CAPABILITIES AND CHARACTER OF INSTRUMENTS}

{II:1}   A

18/4.1917

[side note, rotated: nicht alle diese Bedingungen müssen berücksichtigt werden. Oft genügt eine Auswahl, weil das Instrument nicht exponiert ist, oft weil es durch andere (fähigere) unterstützt]

Instr.

Welche Bedingungen stellen die Instrumente an den Satz?

A Allgemein

    I) Berücksichtigung der *Leisttungsfähigkeit* der Instrumente
        1) die Fähigkeit lange
        2) " Unfähigkeit lange Töne zu erzeugen
        3) " Fähigkeit die langen Töne zu verstärken und abzuschwächen
        4) die Unfähigkeit "   "   "   "   "   "
        5) die Möglichkeit schnelle und langsame Töne deutlich zu bringen
        6) die Schwierigkeiten gewisser Lagen (Ansatz etc) Verbindungen, Bindungen, Sprünge, etc.
        7) die Ausdrucksfähigkeit (das ist die Fähigkeit *p f pp ff sf* etc.,

85 *Instrumentation*

      k) solo instrument with orchestra
      l) the solo within the orchestra
      m) the opera orchestra

—— o ——

Aphoristic: noteworthy phenomena

Are octaves stronger than a unison? Will strong instruments become stronger through doubling? Will strong instruments become stronger through the addition of others?
The solo instr. within the orchestra.
The surrounding instruments.
Concerning clarity (What is it? Its purpose? Its justification? Its technical conditions.) The effect of comfortable and uncomfortable registers. Homogeneous and heterogeneous combinations.
{II:20} Concerning sparse and dense instrumentation. Parts designed for noise, etc.

{ON THE CAPABILITIES AND CHARACTER OF INSTRUMENTS}

{II:1}   A[55]

18/4.1917

| Instr. |

What conditions do instruments impose on a setting?
A General
   1) Consideration of the *performance capabilities* of the instruments
      1) the ability to produce long tones
      2) the inability to produce long tones
      3) the ability   to intensify and weaken long tones
      4) the inability "   "   "   "   "   "
      5) the possibility of producing fast and slow tones clearly
      6) the difficulties of certain registers (attack, etc.), connections, slurs, leaps, etc.
      7) the capacity for expression (that is, the ability to produce *p*, *f*,

It is not necessary to consider these conditions. Often one choice suffices because the instrument is not exposed, often because it is supported by other (more capable) {instruments}

---

55. This letter refers to an indexing system of Schoenberg's; see capital letters in Appendix 1.

86 *Instrumentation*

rasch und deutlich zu bringen und sowohl unvermittelt nebeneinander zu stellen, als sie glatt zu verbinden{)}. Auch die Fähigkeit den Klang vorsätzlich zu ändern!

    8) die Ausgiebigkeit seines Tönes

II. Die *Eigenart* des Instrumentes

    1) Sein Klangcharakter (reich, arm, auffallend, unauffällig, etc)

    2) Sein relativer und absoluter Stärkegrad

        a) in den einzelnen Lagen

        b) in verschiedenen Zeitmassen, Rhymt{h}en

        c) in Sprüngen, etc.

        d) Legato, stacc., etc.

        e) wie verhält sich sein Stärkegrad in der Nachbarschaft anderer z Bsp auffallenderer Instrumente

        f) wie in Mischungen und Mengungen

    3) Sein Umfang

    4) Sonstige Besonderheiten:

        a) Dpf, *pizz, col legno,* etc. Flatterzunge, trem, *Steg,* triller

        b) einzelne fehlende Töne oder Lagen

        c)   ″   Töne die besonders schlecht, gut oder interessant sind.

        d) sonstige Vorzüge oder Nachteile im Vergleich mit dem Durchschnitt

III) *praktische, d.h. materielle (unkünstlerischer) Umstände*

    1) die Seltenheit eines Instrumentes (die höhe Gage des Musikers)

    2) die Grösse des zur Verfügung stehenden Konzert Raumes (etc.)

    3) die Grösse und Qualität vorhandener Orchester oder sonstiger Spieler

    4) die Bestimmung für welchen Spielerkreis das Werk gedacht ist

                      etc.

Literaturbeispiele

%

{II:2}   B) besondere

{I:3}   Instr.   *19/4.1917*

pp, ff, sf, etc. quickly and clearly, both to place them directly next to each other, and to connect them smoothly). Also, the ability to alter the sound quality intentionally!
   8) the richness of its tone
II. The *individuality* of the instrument
   1) the character of its sound (rich, thin, striking, unobtrusive, etc.)
   2) its relative and absolute degree of intensity
      a) in each of its various registers
      b) in different meters, rhythms
      c) in leaps, etc.
      d) legato, staccato, etc.
      e) how its degree of intensity acts in proximity to other, for instance, more striking instruments
      f) how its intensity acts in combinations and mixtures
   3) its range
   4) other features:
      a) Mute, *pizz, col legno,* etc. fluttertongue, *tremolo, sul ponticello,* trills
      b) particular missing tones or registers
      c) particular tones that are especially bad, good, or interesting
      d) other advantages or disadvantages in comparison with the average
III) *practical, i.e., material (inartistic) circumstances*
   1) the rarity of an instrument (the high fee of the musician)
   2) the size of the hall available for the concert (etc.)
   3) the size and quality of existing orchestras and the number and quality of other instrumentalists
   4) consideration for which circle of instrumentalists the work is composed
                                         etc.

examples from the literature

%

{II:2}   B) particulars

{II:3} |Instr.| *19/4.1917*

88 *Instrumentation*

Wovon hängt der Klang eines Satzes (an sich, ohne Rücksicht auf Instrumente) ab?

I) Von der *Anzahl* der Stimmen. Er ist
    a) dicker, wenn viele Stimmen
    b) dünner, "   wenige   "

II)   von den *Lagenverhältnissen* der Stimmen. Er ist
    a) voll, wenn sich in je einer Oktave wenigstens 2 der Stimmen befinden und zwar:
        1) weicher, wenn noch Platz für Akkordtöne ist

        2) härter   "   kein "   "   "   "

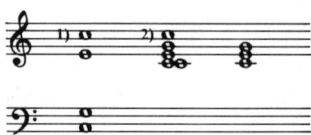

    b) weniger voll, wenn in jeder Oktave bloss eine Stimme sitzt

    c) leer wenn nicht in jeder Oktave eine Stimme sitzt

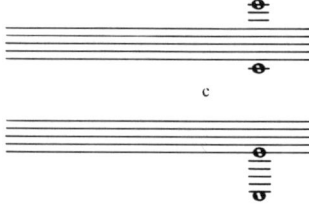

III) Von der *Bewegung* der Stimmen. Sie kann sein:
    1. Alle Stimmen bewegen sich gleichzeitig u.zw.
        a) langsam (choralartig)
        b) bewegt z.Bsp. nach dem Rhythmus einer Gesangsstimme u deren Text
        c) rasch z. Bsp. Beethovens F moll Quart (op 95) letzter Satz Allegro & Coda

89 Instrumentation

Upon what does the sound of a setting (in itself, without regard for instruments) depend?

I) Upon the *number* of parts. It is
    a) fuller if there are many parts
    b) thinner if there are few{er} parts
II) Upon the *registral disposition* of the parts. It is
    a) full, if in each of several octaves there are always at least two voices: specifically:
        1) softer if there is still room for chord tones

        2) harsher if there is no space for chord tones

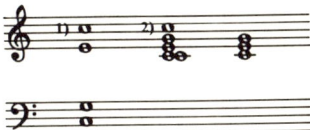

    b) less full if there is only one voice in each octave

    c) empty if there is not a voice in each octave

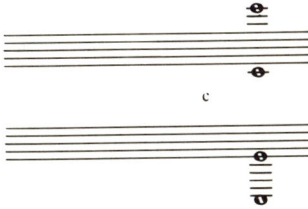

III) On the *motion* of voices. The motion can be:
    1. All voices move simultaneously: specifically:
        a) slowly (like a chorale)
        b) stirringly, e.g., according to the rhythm of a vocal line and its text
        c) quickly, for example, Beethoven F Minor Quartet (op.95) last movement, Allegro & Coda

90 *Instrumentation*

  2. Eine Gruppe von — eine andere
   Stimmen   Gruppe
   bewegt sich   bewegt sich
Melodie { a) langsam — *Harmonie* { — a) rasch } *eine 3te Gruppe*
    b) rasch ——   — b) langs
     ↘c   c c rasch
      ↘d   d d langsam

Literaturbeispiele

  3. Zwei oder mehrere Gruppen von Stimmen bewegen sich so, dass immer eine Bewegung hat, wenn die andere Ruhe hat, so dass die ruhigen Lücken durch die Bewegung ausgefüllt werden

  4. Jede Gruppe oder jede Stimme hat ihre eigene Bewegung

IV. Von einer klangfüllenden Harmonie und deren Lage.
  die kann sein
  1. So wie oft im Klaviersatz
   a) einmal nahe der Melodie
   b) das andere mal nahe dem Bass

  2. Unabhängig von der Oberstimme in einer tieferen Lage, aber im allgemeinen stets in den Bläsern (Hörnersatz bei Wagner)

  3. Weit entfernt von der Hauptstimme
   a) höher als diese
   b) tiefer "   "

[Gehört zum Teil zur Instrumentation!!]

V. Von den Akzenten und sonstigen Betonungsveränderungen (Pausen{)}

VI. Von der Anwendung gewisser aussergewöhnlicher Tonergänzungsmittel: *tremolo, vibrato, tremolo,*[11] Repetition, *stacc, fliegender Bogen, springender Bogen, pizz,* arpeggio, *col legn, am Steg,* Dämpfer, Flatterzunge, Triller, Verzierungen.

VII. Von der Verwendung von charakteristischen (z. Bsp natur nachahmenden) Stimmen und Figuren

19/4.1917

Besprechung der Eigentümlichkeiten der Instrumente

1. Gattung, Konstruction, Spielart, Geschichtliches in Kürze, aus Berlioz citieren und anderen Nachschlagwerken.

---

11. Schoenberg inadvertently repeats "tremolo."

91 *Instrumentation*

2. One group of voices — another group

melody { a) slowly ⎯⎯
b) fast ⎯
  ↘ c
  ↘ d } *Harmony* { ⎯ a) fast
⎯ b) slowly
c
d } *a 3d group*
c fast
d slowly

examples from the literature

3. Two or more groups of voices move so that one is always in motion when the other is at rest, so that quiet gaps are filled up by motion
4. Each group or each voice has its own motion

{II:4}   IV. One full-sounding harmony and its register, which can be
   1. As often in a piano setting
      a) one time near the melody
      b) another time near the bass
   2. Independent of the upper voice in a lower register but in general always in the winds (horn settings in Wagner)
   3. Far removed from the main voice
      a) higher than the main voice
      b) lower than   "   "   "

Belongs to the part concerning instrumentation!!

V. Upon accents and changes of emphasis (rests)
VI. Upon the use of certain unusual means of tonal definition: *tremolo, vibrato, tremolo,* repetition, *staccato, sautillé, jeté, pizz.,* arpeggio, *col legno, sul ponticello,* mute, fluttertongue, trills, embellishments.
VII. Upon the use of characteristic (e.g., imitating nature) voices and figures

{II:5}   19/4.1917

Discussion of the Characteristics of Instruments

1.   Family, construction, method of playing, history in brief, citing from Berlioz and other reference works.

In diesem Kapitel soll die Beschreibung der Technik so ausführlich wie möglich sein, um späteren Zeiten Aufschluss zu geben, über die Leistungs-fähigkeit unserer Instrumente.

    II. Umfang
   III. Lagen und deren Charakteristik (Charakteristik des Tons)
   IV. Die Technik
      1. Tonerzeugung (leicht, schwer?)
      2. Gehaltene und schnelle Noten (Grad der Beweglichkeit)
      3. cresc u. dim.
         a) wie gross ist der Unterschied zwischen *p* u *pp*, *p* u *f*, *f* u *ff* etc
         b) ist   die An- und Abschwellung leicht oder schwer?
            geht   "   "   "   "   langsam oder schnell?
            so schnell   "   "   "   "   ? (zBsp cresc in schnellen Noten?)
         c) wie verhalten sich die Stärkegrade bei rascher und bei langsamer Bewegung{?}
         d) wie verhalten sich die Stärkegrade u die Schwellungen zu einigen anderen durchschnittlichen Instrumenten?
         e) ist das Instrument fähig scharfe Akzente zu bringen?
         f) ist das Instrument fähig sehr zart zu spielen (und auch: zurückzutreten?)?
    V. Wie verhält sich das Instrument in der Nachbarschaft anderer? Nimmt es Farbe und Stärke an, oder giebt es ab? Wem? Wem nicht?
   VI. Für welche Arten *solistischen* Ausdrucks wurde das Instrument in der Literatur verwendet? Ist es an diese Verwendung gebunden? (begrenzt). (Beispiele{})}
  VII. Welche Rolle spielt das Instrument gewöhnlich im
      1) dünnen Satz;
      2) Halb-Tutti;
      3) vollen Tutti.   (Beispiele)
 VIII. Wie verhält es sich in Mischungen a2, a3, a4 etc (Systematisch alle Mischungen!)
   IX. Wie verhält es sich als Oberstimme wenn andere Instrumente das gleiche
                          " Mittelstimme {wenn} die anderen Stimmen haben
                                  " Bass
                             lagenweise besprechen und mit Rücksicht auf Bewegung und Stärke

93 *Instrumentation*

> In this chapter the description of technique should be as detailed as possible in order to give later periods information about the efficiency of our instruments.

II. Range
III. Registers and their characteristics (characteristics of tone)
IV. Technique
    1. Tone production (easy, difficult?)
    2. held and fast notes (degree of agility)
    3. cres. and dim.
        a) how great the difference is between *p* and *pp*, *p* and *f*, *f* and *ff*, etc.
        b) is the swelling and subsiding easy or difficult?
            does " " " " occur slowly or quickly?
            how fast " " " " ? (for example, cresc. in fast notes?)
        c) how does the degree of intensity fare in faster and slower motion?
        d) how do intensity and swellings act in relation to several other, average instruments?
        e) is the instrument capable of producing sharp accents?
        f) is the instrument capable of playing very delicately (and also, of receding?)
V. How does the instrument act in proximity to others? Does it take on color and intensity, or does it pass on these qualities? To which instrument? To which not?
VI. For what kinds of *soloistic* expression was the instrument used in the literature? Is it restricted to this use? (limited). (Examples)
VII. Which role does the instrument usually play in
    1) a thin setting
    2) half-tutti;
    3) full-tutti. (Examples)
VIII. How does it behave in combinations a2, a3, a4, etc. (Systematically all combinations!)
IX. How does it act as an upper voice when other instruments play the same.
How does it act as a middle voice when other instruments play the other voices.
How does it act as a bass
        discuss registrally and with concern for
        motion and intensity

94 *Instrumentation*

{1:24}   *15/IV.1917*

Über:

Instrumente

für fast alle Instrumente gelten folgende Beobachtungen:
Es macht grosse Schwierigkeiten

1. einen Ton länger gleich stark zu halten
2.   "   " anschwellen zu lassen
3.   "   " *rasch* zum Klingen zu bringen
4.   "   " sehr leise klingen zu lassen
5. Töne der
   - a) äussersten Grenzen (Höhe, Tiefe) schwierig aber ausgiebig
   - b) Mittellage {sind} gewöhnlich leicht aber unergiebig

———

Die meisten Instrumente trachten auf irgendeine Art das Erloschene oder im Erlöschen begriffene Leben des Tones wieder anzufachen solche Mittel sind:

    das Vibrato (der Geigen, Flöten Gesang etc) (*Schwebung*)
    " Tremolo   "   "   "   Klavier
    die Repetition
    der Triller, Mordent etc. ♩♩♩♩ ♩♩♩♩

Im weiteren Verlauf führen diese Methoden dazu, möglichst viele kleine Noten zu verwenden.

Die Orgel, deren Töne nur stärker oder schwächer werden können, benützt Schweberegister etc.

— o —

Man kann im Sinne der obigen Eigenschaften die Instrumente einteilen in

1) solche mit kurzlebigem Ton (Klavier, Harfe, Xylophon, Guitarre, Glockenspiel, Pauke etc.)
2) solche mit langlebigem Ton
   - a) mit Vibrato etc
   - b) ohne   "   etc

{1:25} Welches sind *die Erfordernisse eines guten Klangs*

{1:24}   15/IV.1917

About:
Instruments

The following observations are valid for almost all instruments:
It is very difficult to
1. prolong a tone at one level of intensity
2. produce a crescendo
3. make a tone speak *quickly*
4. produce a tone very softly
5. Tones of
    a) the most extreme ranges (high, low) are difficult but rich
    b) the middle range are usually easy but unproductive

———

Most instruments try in some way to reanimate the expired or expiring vitality of the tone
such means are:

vibrato (violins, flutes, singing, etc.)	(*vibration*)
tremolo " "	piano
repetition	
trill, mordent etc. ♪♪♪♪ ♪♪♪♪	

In the further course of events, these methods lead to using as many notes of small value as possible.

The organ, whose tones can only become stronger or weaker, uses tremolo stops, etc.

— o —

In terms of the above-mentioned characteristics, instruments can be classified as
1) those with a tone of short duration (piano, harp, xylophone, guitar, glockenspiel, kettledrum, etc.)
2) those with a tone of long duration
    a) with vibrato, etc.
    b) without vibrato, etc.

{1:25}   What are *the requirements of good sound*?

96 *Instrumentation*

> 16/4.1917

    I. Deutlichkeit
a) des Ganzen insofern 2) die Hauptsachen sich von den Nebensachen unterscheiden sollen
    1. der Charakter des Ganzen und jeder Einzelhcit ihrer Bedeutung entsprechend, zur Geltung kommen sollen
  b) der Haupt und Nebenstimmen und zwar in Hinsicht auf ihre{n}
    1) melodischen Inhalt u. Charakter
    2) rhyt{h}mischen " " "
    3) harmonischen " " "
    4) dynamischen " " "
  II. Möglichst vollkommene Uebereinstimmung zwischen den von den Ausführungs-Instrumenten geforderten Leistungen und ihrer Eignung und Fähigkeit dazu.
  III. Verhältnismässig einfache Anlage.
  IV. Einheitlichkeit und Mannigfaltigkeit

Was ist Wohlklang?

Wohlklang ist (unter den Erfordernissen eines guten Klanges wurde er nicht erwähnt, weil er mit dem guten Klang identisch ist) soweit sein Zustandekommen nicht durch die Punkte I–IV („Erfordernisse eines guten Klangs") garantiert ist, eine teils im jeweiligen Zeitgeschmack begründete Eigentümlichkeit des Klanges. Zum anderen Teil ist er in unserem Gehör begründet und verändert sich ebenso, wie dieses.

—— o ——

{1:23}   In die *Instrumentationslehre* gehört auch folgendes: Klavier Auszüge, 2hdg, 4hdg, etc.
  andere Bearbeitungen
    Arrangements
    Retouchen
usw   Instrumentations-Änderungen bei älteren und jüngeren Komp.-(Stil etc)
Um Instrumentierung klassischer Werke, und solche von Bach, Händel etc.

> 16/4.1917

I. Clarity
   a) of the whole, insofar as 2) the main ideas are to be distinguished from the subsidiary ones
      1. the character of the whole, and of each detail in keeping with their importance, should get their due
   b) of the main and subordinate voices, particularly with regard to their
      1) melodic content and character
      2) rhythmic   "   "   "
      3) harmonic   "   "   "
      4) dynamic   "   "   "
II. As far as possible, complete agreement between the output demanded of the performing instruments and their suitability and capability for that purpose
III. Relatively simple design
IV. Uniformity and diversity

<u>*What is euphony?*</u>

Euphony (not mentioned under the requirements of a good sound because it is synonymous with it), inasmuch as its occurrence is not guaranteed by points I–IV ("Requirements of a good sound"), is a characteristic of sound based partly on the taste of any given era. For the rest, it is based on our hearing and changes just as our hearing changes.

— o —

{1:23} The following is also part of the *Instruction in Instrumentation*: piano arrangements, 2 hands, 4 hands, etc.
   other settings
      arrangements
      reworkings
etc. Changes in instrumentation of older and newer compositions (style, etc.)
Reinstrumentation of classical works, and those by Bach, Handel, etc.

98 *Instrumentation*

zu *Klav.Ausz*: eine gewisse Zeit hat hat {sic} damit gerechnet, dass Klav.Ausz. nur ungenau gespielt werden. Der Klav.Ausz-Stil dieser Zeit ist daher orchestral. (Daher kam es auch, dass es damals soviele Musiker gab, die nicht gut Klavier spielten - es war nicht unbedingt nötig) Jetzt beginnt man wieder genau zu spielen und kann daher wieder einen wirklichen Klav.Ausz-Stil finden.

{TRANSPOSITION}

{II:12}   21.4.1917

Instr

Die Frage der *transponierenden Instrumente* könnte folgendermassen gelöst werden:

Der Hornist (oder Trp-er oder Cl-ist) lerne als C-Dur-Skala *nicht* die Tonart spielen, bei der er kein Ventil oder Ventil[12] betätigt, (wie es bis jetzt geschieht) sondern diejenige, die wirklich C-Dur klingt. Dementsprechend alle Tonarten weiter ebenso.

Es ist eine rein formalistische Ueberlegung, die zu dem entgegengesetzten Vorzug geführt hat: man sagt; C-Dur sei jene Tonart, die kein Vorzeichen hat, also müsste das unveränderte Naturweise der C-Dur ohne Klappen und Ventile benützt werden. Praktisch aber ist es ohne Belang, ob ein Gericht das C-Dur oder F nennt, denn schliesslich sind es nur Namen; und wenn die einen, die ich vorschlage, mit der Natur des Instruments nicht übereinstimmen, so stimmen die anderen mit der Wirklichkeit des wahren Klanges nicht überein, was ärger ist und grosse Schwierigkeiten verursacht hat.

Um ein Beispiel zu geben, wird also ein Hornist auf dem F-Horn ohne Ventil blasen, wenn die Noten f g a b c d e dort stehen; bekommt er ein B-Horn, so hat er (ebenso wie der Geiger, wenn er eine Viola in die Hand nimmt, oder der Cellist, der ja viererlei Schlüssel lesen muss: 𝄢 𝄡 und 𝄞 den letzten in 2 Formen) ein anderes Instrument,

{II:13}   das einen anderen Schlüssel hat und spielt nun ohne Ventil, wenn er die Noten b c d es f g a vor sich hat. Es kommen also für den Hornisten

---

12. "Ventile."

Concerning *piano arrangements*: A certain era took into account that piano arrangements are consistently played inaccurately. For this reason, the style of piano arrangements of that era is orchestral. (This is also why there were at that time so many musicians who did not play the piano well — it was not absolutely necessary). We are now beginning to play accurately again, and can therefore find a genuine piano reduction style.[56]

{TRANSPOSITION}[57]

{II:12}   21.4.1917

Instr.

The question of the *transposing instruments* could be solved as follows:

In learning the C major scale, the horn player (or trumpeter or clarinetist) should *not* play the key in which no valves are depressed (as has been the practice until now), but should use instead the key that really sounds C major. Accordingly, the same applies for all other keys.

It is a purely formalistic consideration that has led to the opposite preference. It is said that C major is the key that has no signature, therefore the unchanged essence of C major, without stops and valves, should be used. But in practical terms it is irrelevant whether there is a judgment made calling that C major or F, because ultimately they are merely names; and if the ones I propose do not accord with the nature of the instrument, the others do not accord with the reality of the true sound, which is worse and has caused great difficulties.

To give an example, a horn player will blow into the F horn without depressing valves if the notes to be played are f g a b c d e; if he is given a B♭ horn, he is like the violinist when he picks up a viola, or the cellist (who in fact must learn to read clefs of different kinds: 𝄢 𝄡 and 𝄞 the last in 2 forms) a different instrument

{II:13}   with a different clef, and can now play without valves if he sees the notes b c d e♭ f g a in front of him. For horn players, at most, there remain ad-

---

56. Compare Schoenberg, *Style*, 348–49.

57. See ibid., 343–44.

höchstens noch Es und B {illegible}-Hörner in Betracht. Und selbst die werden kaum wirklich gespielt, sondern sind meist nur eine Notierungs-Marotte.

Der Klarinettist ist insofern weniger günstig dran, als es hier mehr Stimmungen giebt. Im allgemeinen aber ist ein Klarinettist selten nebenbei auch auf allen Instrumenten zu Hause, spielt selten nebenbei Bss Cl., Es-, D- und Ao Kl. Da die Bss-Kl heute nur mehr in B gebaut wird, eine der beiden hohen Kl. (Es oder D) vielleicht entbehrlich wird, so hat der universellste Klarinettist 3–5 verschiedene Instrumente, resp Schlüssel zu lernen, was immer noch leichter ist, als eine oder zwei Transpositionen, die er ja sowieso lernen muss.

—— o ——

{EXERCISES}

{II:7}   20/4.1917

Aufgabenbuch zur Instrumentationslehre

1. Partitur Auszüge (eventuell bloss Partien oder Stellen) aus klassischen und modernen Werken in Violin u. Bass Schlüssel in 3–6 Zeilen (ohne Nennung der Instrumentennamen{)}.

2. Klavier-Stücke   in Stimmen aufgelöst ⎫
   Kammer Werke   "   "   "   ⎬ ebenso dargestellt
                                           ⎭

Der Schüler kann jedes solcher Beispiele (es wird angegeben für welche *Besetzung das Stück sich eignet*, für welche nicht) in *verschiedenen Besetzungen* ausarbeiten.

Er kann hier auch lernen: *disponieren*

Ferner: Instrumentations Uebung, indem er in diesen Auszug die Namen der Instrumente einträgt (er kann es auch ausschreiben)

(Eventuell auch ein Heft: *Lösungen*{,} in welchem für alle oder einen Teil der Beispiele, von manchem mehrere, Ausführungen gegeben werden)

{I:32}   22/4.1917   *Aufgaben zur Inst. Variationen für Klavier von Beethoven, Brahms* etc könnten so (eventuell sehr fein) bearbeitet werden, dass eine Anzahl *instrumentierbarer Stimmen* vorliegt. — Ebenso andere *Klavierwerke*. Besonders wäre auch an *Geigen u. Vcl Sonaten, Trios* etc. zu denken; ebenso an *Gesang u Kl*.

ditionally only horns in E♭ and B♭ {illegible}; and even these will hardly ever really be played, since most often their use is merely a notational fad.

The clarinetist is in this respect in a less favorable position, as there are several tunings. In general, however, a clarinetist is seldom comfortable on all instruments, and seldom plays bass clarinet, E♭, D, and alto clarinet. As the bass clarinet is nowadays built only in B♭, and one of the two high clarinets (E♭ or D) can probably be dispensed with, so the most all-encompassing clarinetist has to learn 3–5 different instruments and their methods of notation, which is nonetheless easier than one or two transpositions that he must learn anyway.

—— o ——

{EXERCISES}

{II:7}   20/4.1917

Exercise book for the Instruction in Instrumentation
   1. Excerpts from scores (possibly merely sections or places) from classical and modern works in the treble and bass clefs on 3–6 staves (without mention of the names of the instruments).
   2. Piano pieces   reduced to parts ⎱
      Chamber works   "   "   ⎰ presented similarly

The student can work out each such example (it is indicated for which *instrumentation the piece is suited*, for which not) in <u>*various scorings*</u>.

He can also here learn to *dispose* instruments properly on the page.

Further: Instrumentation exercise by entering in this excerpt the names of the instruments (he can also write it out)

(Possibly a notebook: <u>*solutions*</u> in which realizations are provided for all or a part of the examples; in some instances, several realizations)

{I:32}   22/4.1917   *Exercise in Instrumentation: variations for piano by Beethoven, Brahms*, etc. could be arranged (perhaps in great detail) so long as a number of *voices suitable for instrumentation* are present. — The same with other *piano works, sonatas for violin and for cello, trios*, etc. should particularly be kept in mind; likewise *voice and piano*.

{Formenlehre}

{II:10}   20/4.1917

Zur Formenlehre
Die ersten Anweisungen über den (motivischen) Aufbau und die Organisation von Gedanken finden sich bereits im Kontrapunkt. Daher kann die *Formenlehre* sich darauf beschränken, auf das dort gesagte zu verweisen und es bloss kurz zu rekapitulieren (Es ist ja auch selbstverständlich, dass ein Schüler, der selbständige Stimmen schreiben soll, schon genug dergl. weiss) (Im Kontrapunkt werden auch Sätzchen gebildet, die sich auf die Harmonielehre berufen.) *Die Formenlehre beginnt daher mit den Formen.*
    Versuch einer Einteilung
I. Sätze

1. Sätze
{
  1. zweiteilige Gebilde und Formen (erst solche mit Taktpaaren Vieren, dann ungerade)
    a) symmetrische (dazu Perioden etc. eventuell auch Sequenzen und andere Wiederholungen{})
    b) annähernd symetrische (Abweichungen von der Symetrie{})
      (dazu event. auch Gänge etc)
    c) unsymetrische
  2. einteilige (ungeteilte Gebilde und Formen)
}
3. drei- und mehrteilige Gebilde und Formen
4. zusammengesetzte Formen (die noch nicht das 2- oder 3-teilige Lied sind{,} aber dennoch aus mehreren aneinander gereihten Ideen bestehen (Satzkette{,} Nachsätze, etc) *Beiordnung von Ideen*
5. Zusammengesetzte, mehrteilige Formen deren Nebenteile einem Hauptteil untergeordnet sind:

%

{II:11}
    a) dreiteiliges Lied
    b) zwei " "

{Instruction in Form}

{II:10}   20/4.1917

Concerning the Instruction in Form[58]
The first instructions about the (motivic) construction and the organization of ideas are already contained in the counterpoint {text}. Therefore the *Instruction in Form* can be restricted to referring to what was stated there, merely recapitulating it briefly. (It is obvious by now that a student who is supposed to write independent voices already knows enough about such matters.) (In counterpoint, small phrases are constructed, as based on the theory of harmony.) *The Instruction in Form therefore begins with forms.*

Attempt at a classification

1st movements:
1. two-part structures and forms (first with measure pairings in four, then with uneven measures)
   a) symmetrical ones (in addition, periods, etc.; possibly also sequences and other repetitions)
   b) approximately symmetrical ones (deviations from symmetry (in addition, possibly, also transitions)
   c) asymmetrical ones
2. one-part (undivided structures and forms)
3. structures and forms of three or more parts

4. compound forms (which are not yet the 2- or 3-part song form but that nevertheless consist of several ideas arranged in a series (phrase chain, closing statements, etc.) *Coordination of ideas*
5. compound forms of several parts whose subordinate parts are governed by one main part:

%

{II:11}   a) three-part song
          b) two-   "   "

---

58. The method outlined below, working from the writing of small phrases to pieces, is realized in *Fundamentals of Musical Composition*.

zum 3 teiligen Lied:
   der *Mittelteil*   a) die Durchführung   } eines Gedankens
                          b) die Auflösung

NB. Woher kommt das: Jedes Thema oder Motiv verliert bei der Auflösung an Besonderheit (harmonisch u rhyt{h}misch) wird allgemeiner und endet schliesslich in einem Gebilde von verhältnismässig uncharakteristischer Gestalt (Nachweis an Notenbeispielen)

  Welches ist der Sinne der Durchführung?   A̲ ?
  *   "   "   "   "   Auflösung?*   A̲ ?
  Die Methoden der Durchführung und Auflösung   A̲ ?
  Die Entstehung des Mittelteils

Ein musikalischer Gedanke, um Eindruck zu machen, erfasst zu werden (er geht vorüber und steht nicht, wie bei den Malern beständig vor Augen) muss (oft) wiederholt werden (Strophenlied!) So kann man sich die einfachste grössere Form als oftmalige Wiederholung eines Gedankens vorstellen (z Bsp eines Tanzliedes). Um Abwechslung zu erhalten mögen da Zwischenspiele gemacht worden sein, die sollten schliesslich mit einem Doppelpunkt zur Wiederholung münden. Dies {ist} der Ursprung des II. Teils. — <u>*Die 2-teilige Form könnte entstanden*</u> sein aus dem Solo-(Vorsänger) mit dem Chor-(Refrain) Auch der Tanz mit Chor-(Refrain) kann sein Ursprung sein. — (Jedenfalls wird es gut sein 2- und 3-teilige Formen auseinanderzuhalten{)}}

{I:27}   17.4.1917

Aufgabe der *Formenlehre*: eine möglichst grosse Anzahl erprobter Anwendungsprinzipien und Formschemata in einheitlicher Darstellung auf möglichst allgemeinen Grundsätzen basierend für die kleinsten bis zu den grössten Formen darzubieten.

20/4.1917

  Die Symetrie als eines der Formprinzipien
    auch unsymetrische Formen beruhen oft auf der Symetrie: die Abweichungen von der Symetrie

for the 3-part song:

the *middle section*   a) the elaboration[59] } of an idea
b) the dissolution

NB. How is it that: in undergoing dissolution, every theme or motive loses individuality (harmonic and rhythmic), becomes more ordinary, and ends up as a structure with relatively uncharacteristic features{?} (Reference to musical examples)

What is the meaning of elaboration?	A| ?[60]
" " " " " *dissolution?*	A| ?
The methods of elaboration and dissolution	A| ?

The formation of the middle section

In order for a musical idea to make an impression, to be comprehended (it passes by and does not remain, as painters' works do, constantly before their eyes); it must (often) be repeated (strophic lied!). Thus the simplest larger form can be imagined as the frequent repetition of an idea (for example, a dance song). To obtain variety, interludes can be composed that should ultimately lead to a double bar for the repetition. This is the origin of part II. — <u>The 2-part form may have originated from</u> the solo (main soloist) with chorus (refrain) Also the dance with chorus (refrain) may be its origin. — (In any case, it will be good to distinguish between 2- and 3-part forms.)

17.4.1917

Goal of the *Instruction in Form:* to offer, in integrated presentation, an optimally large number of proven principles of application and diagrams of form, based on the most general possible principles, suitable for use in creating forms of the smallest to the largest size.

20/4.1917

Symmetry as one of the principles of form
even unsymmetrical forms are often based on symmetry: deviations from symmetry

---

59. Schoenberg preferred the translation of *Durchführung* as "elaboration." See Schoenberg, *Fundamentals*, 151.

60. I.e. "Antwort" {"answer"}.

— o —

Die Formenlehre wird vielleicht mit einem Kapitel (nach den Einleitungen in denen der Begriff der Form definiert und die Methode des Buches bekannt wird) beginnen, das den Titel führt: *„Die Entstehung der musikalischen Formen"*

oder besser:
„Wie man sich die musikalischen Formen entstanden denken könnte," das sollte soweit wie möglich durchgeführt werden.

— o —

Auf welchen Zusammenhängen begründet sich die Wirkung und Fasslichkeit des *Recitativs*?

— o —

{1:22} Die Ausnützung der Zusammenhänge zu dem Zwecke der Entwicklung, Fortsetzung, Verbindung, Ueberleitung, Kontrastierung, etc gehört in die *Formenlehre*.

— o —

The *Instruction in Form* will perhaps begin (after introductions in which the concept of form is defined and the methodology of the book is revealed) with a chapter entitled: *"The Origin of Musical Forms"*
or better:
"How one could imagine the genesis of musical forms." This should be carried out as far as possible.

— o —

Which relationships form the basis for the effect and comprehensibility of *recitatives*?

— o —

{1:22} Taking advantage of connectives for the purpose of elaboration, continuation, connection, transition, contrasting, etc. is part and parcel of the *Instruction in Form*.

Appendix 1

A Transcription and Translation of Schoenberg's Indexes

The following lists are a transcription and translation of Schoenberg's two indexes for ZKIF, which define the topics discussed in the two notebooks housing the original manuscript. In each notebook an index appears before the body of text.

ABBREVIATIONS

Aufg.	Aufgaben
Dispos.	Disposition
f.	für
Formenl.	Formenlehre
Kontrap.	kontrapuntische
Ktrpkt., Ktrp.	Kontrapunkt
Instr., Inst., Instru.	Instrumentation
u.	und
Zusammenhg., Zshg.	Zusammenhang

110 *Appendix 1*

INDEX TO NOTEBOOK I

{cover}   Zusammenhang, Kontrapunkt, Instrumentation, Formenlehre   Heft 1

{inside cover}   registriert bis Seite 32

{flyleaf}   Durchschriften unter Doubletten

{i}   *Register*

Ktrpkt. 2/3, 4, 5, 6, 7, 8, 16, 17, 18, 19, 28, 30, 32

Instr. 24, 25

Zusammenhang: Seite 1 (Fasslichkeit) 4,5, (Motiv) 6,7,8 (Rhyt{h}mus) 9, 10, 11, 12, 13, 14, 15, 16, 17, 18, 19, 20, 21, 22, 28, 29, 30, 31, 27, 33, 34, 35, 36

Formenlehre, 22, 27

Aufgaben f. Inst. 32

{ii}
    A   Aesthetik 15
           Ausnützung des Zshg. 22
           Aufgaben f. Inst. 32

    B   Bedürfnis des Motivs 2
           Bedeutsamkeit 21

    C   Charakteristik 30

    D   Deutlichkeit 21

    E   Einheitlichkeit 18
           Entwicklung 2, 22

    F   Fasslichkeit 1, 3, 4, 4, 5, 20, 27
           Füllstimme 2
           Formbildende Prinzipien 10, 11, 16, 17
           Formenlehre 22
                "   Aufgabe der 27
                "   Einleitung 27

    G   Gliederung 6, 14
           Gegensatz 13, 14, 22
           Gesetze mehrere im Thema 31

    H   Haupt u. Nebensachen 14

    I

    K   Kontrap. Aufg. 16, 32
           Klang Erfordernisse des 25
           Kadenzen melodische 19, 28

Schoenberg's Indexes

INDEX TO NOTEBOOK I

{cover}   Coherence, Counterpoint, Instrumentation, Instruction in Form, Book 1

{inside cover}   indexed up through page 32

{flyleaf}   carbons with duplicates

{i}   *Index*

Counterpoint 2/3, 4, 5, 6, 7, 8, 16, 17, 18, 19, 28, 29, 30, 32

Instrumentation 24, 25

Coherence page 1 (comprehensibility) 4,5, (motive) 6,7,8 (rhythm) 9, 10, 11, 12, 13, 14, 15, 16, 17, 18, 19, 20, 23, 24, 28, 29, 30, 31, 27, 33, 34, 35, 36

Instruction in Form, 22, 27

Exercises for Instrumentation 32

{ii}   A[1]   Ability to be surveyed 4
            Aesthetics 15
            Articulation 6, 14

      C   Cadences, melodic 19, 28
            Characteristics 30
            Clarity 25
            Coherence 21, 21, 22, 27, 33, 34, 35, 36
            Comprehensibility 1, 2, 4, 4, 5, 20, 27
            Connections 13
            Contrapuntal exercises 16, 32
            Contrast 13, 14, 22

      D   Development 2, 22
            Difficulties of the Instruments 24

      E   Euphony 25

      F   Filler voice 2

      I   Independent voice 2
            Instruction in Form 22
               "   "   "   Task of 27
               "   "   "   Introduction 27
            Instrumentation Exercises 32

      K   Key, expressing 17
            "   retaining 18, 19
            "   abandoning 19
            "   stating 18, 19

---

1. Because the list of topics is here alphabetized in English, it does not correspond directly to the German transcription.

L

M melodisch 3, 4
Motiv 5, 6, 7, 8, 9, 10, 11, 12, 13
Mannigfaltigkeit 18

N

O

P Prinzipien formbildende 10, 11, 16, 17
" zusammenhaltende 28, 29, 30, 32
" auseinandertreibende 28, 29, 30, 32

Qu

R Rhythmus 8, 9, 28, 29, 30, 32
Recitativ 27

S Selbständige Stimme 2
Schulform 15
Skala 19
Schwierigkeiten der Instrumente 24
Symetrie 27

T Takt 28, 29, 30, 32
Tonart ausdrücken 17
" festhalten 18, 19
" verlassen 19
" angeben 18, 19
Tonbelebung 24
Tondauer 24

U Ueberblickbar 4,
Ursprünge der Rhythmen 33

V Variierung 12, 13, 22 (?)
Verbindungen 13
Vermittelndes 13

W Wiederholung 11, 12, 13
Wohlklang

X

Y

Z Zusammenhg. 20, 21, 22, 27, 33, 34, 35, 36

{cover}   **B. INDEX TO NOTEBOOK II**   ⑨[2]

    L   Laws, several in a theme 31

    M   Main and subordinate ideas 14
          Mediations 13
          melodic 3, 4
          Meter 28, 29, 30, 32
          Motive 5, 6, 7, 8, 9, 10, 11, 12, 13

    O   Obligation of the motive 2
          Origins of rhythm 33

    P   Principles, structuring 10, 11, 16, 17
               "   holding together 28, 29, 30, 32
               "   driven apart 28, 29, 30, 32

    R   Recitative 27
          Repetition 11, 12, 13
          Rhythm 8, 9, 28, 30, 32

    S   Scale 19
          School form 15
          Signification 21
          Sound, requirement of 25
          Structural principles 10, 11, 16, 17
          Symmetry 27

    T   Tone animation 24
          Tone duration 24

    U   Uniformity 18
          Use of Coherence 22

    V   Variation 12, 13

    W

    X

    Y

    Z

---

2. The circled "9" refers to the catalogue number of this manuscript on Schoenberg's list "Unfinished Theoretical Manuscripts."

Appendix 1

	A, D, E[3]	Instru. Lehre	
	B	Aufg " "	
	C	Formenlehre	
	F, G, H	Zusammenhang	

Durchschrift von Seite 1–21/22 unter Doubletten

{i}
- A   Ähnlichkeit 29
       Aufg. Buch z.Instr. 7
- B
- C
- D   Dispos. Instrum: 14–20
       "   Formenl: 10, 11
       "   Zshg: 21, 22
       "   Ktrp:
- E
- F   Formenlehre 10, 11
- G
- H
- I   *Instrumentation* 1, 2, 3, 4, 5, 7, 8, 12, 13, 14, 15, 16, 18, 19, 20
- J
- K   Kontrapunkt 9
- L

{ii}
- M
- N
- O
- P
- Q
- R
- S
- T
- U
- V   Vorwort: 9

---

3. These letters correspond to tabs inserted into the manuscript.

B. INDEX TO NOTEBOOK II

A, D, E

B   Book of exercises for the Instruction in Instrumentation

C   Coherence

F, G, H

             Instruction in Form
             Instruction in Instrumentation

Carbon from pages 1–21/22
with duplicates

A	Arrangement of Instrumentation:		14–20
	"	" Instruction in Form:	10, 11
	"	" Coherence:	21, 22
	"	" Counterpoint:	

B   Book of exercises for the Instruction in Instrumentation 7

C   Coherence: 21, 22, 49 {*sic*} 29
            Counterpoint 9

D

E

F   Foreword: 9

G

H

I   Instruction in Form 10, 11
            Instrumentation 1, 2, 3, 4, 5, 7, 8, 12, 13, 14, 15, 16, 18, 19, 20

J

K

L

M

N

O

P

Q

R

S   Similarity, 29

T

U
V
W
X
Y
Z   Zusammenhang: 21, 22, 49 29

W
X
Y
Z

Appendix 2

A Table of Contents for Each Notebook of ZKIF

Below I have compiled a table of contents for each notebook of ZKIF. The lists show the order in which the text of ZKIF appears in its manuscript form. Later Schoenberg catalogued the contents of each notebook in the two indexes reproduced in Appendix 1.

NOTEBOOK I

   1. *Zusammenhang, Kontrapunkt, Instrumentation, Formenlehre*

Index	*Unnumbered*
"Theory of coherence"	1
"In contrast to *ripieno* or filler-voices"	2
"What are the requirements of a) *the comprehensible*"	4
"What is a motive?"	6
"What is rhythm?"	8
"Structuring principles"	10
"Articulation"	14
"Conditions for the first exercise in counterpoint"	16
"Underlying the following inquiries and statements"	20
"The following is also part of the *Instruction in Instrumentation*"	23
"Instruments"	24
"Task of the *Instruction in Form*"	27
"Almost every theme proves to be"	31
"First exercise in counterpoint"	32
"Exercises in instrumentation"	32

"Artistically usable coherence"	33
"Second outline for *Zusammenhang*"	35

II. *Notenbeispiele zu Kontrapunkt, Formenlehre, Instrumentation u. Zusammenhang*

"In relation to counterpoint"	1

NOTEBOOK II

Index	*Unnumbered*
"What conditions do the instruments make on a piece"	1
"Upon what does the sound of a composition depend"	3
"Discussion of the characteristics of instruments"	5
"Exercise Book for the *Instruction in Instrumentation*"	7
"Foreword"	9
"Outline for *Instruction in Form*"	10
"Transposing instruments"	12
"Outline for *Instrumentation*"	14
"First outline for *Zusammenhang*"	21
"Understanding — recognition of similarity"	35

Appendix 3

Two Bibliographic Lists Compiled by Schoenberg

The transcriptions below preserve Schoenberg's own spacing and punctuation. The first list, "Unfinished Theoretical Works," is catalogued as number T37.1 at the Arnold Schoenberg Institute. Compiled in the 1940s, it is Schoenberg's only attempt to list separately his theoretical works. The second list, *"Manuscripts,* Mostly (Real Manuscripts) Handwritten, Some Perhaps Unpublished, Some Fragments," which also contains some theoretical works, is catalogued as number T20.1. It appears to have been typed on the same machine as "Unfinished Theoretical Works," thus suggesting a post-1940 date.

Abbreviations: Ged. = Gedanke   Orch. = Orchestra   Str. = Streich   u. = und

LIST ONE

UNFINISHED THEORETICAL WORKS
(also including polemics and short remarks)

1)	A "Theory" of Fourths (fragment, to Tovey{)}	1939??
2)	Outlines of theories: counterpoint 11 sheets, instrumentation (1) Gesetze, Regeln, Lehresätze, Definitionen (4)	
3)	Four independent fragments attempting: Aa Der musikalische Gedanke and seine Darstellung, 9 sheets, 9 copies Ab Gedanke (2) Ba Ged. u. Darst. (9 pages) Bb Zusammenhang (9 pages, 9 copies)	
4)	Kontrapunkt 19 Seiten handschr und 3 Seiten Noten Fragment, begonnen	29/9.1926
5)	Counterpoint, a textbook, fragment begun November	1936

6)		Ueber Verzierungen, Neger-, Zigeuner- und andere primitive Rhythmen und Vogelgesang Durchschlag (carbon copy) siehe:	1922
7)		Kleine Manuscripte	
8)		ein Buch, enthaltend Zusammenhang, Kontrapunkt, Instrumentation, Formenlehre, 35 Seiten und zahlreiche Notenbeispiele	1917
11)		Aufgaben zur Instrumentation (Seite 1–23) Gebrauchsanweisung: p.30; Vorwort, p.31–35	1917
12)		Mahler's IX. Symphonie (3 Seiten)	1917
13)		Neufassung der Harmonielehre A (1–6) B (1–3)	about 1937
14)		4 Fragments: A) Manners of Constructing a Phrase (7) B) Criterions {*sic*} of Value (B1:3; B2:1) C) Competition of musical knowledge (4) D) Musical Examples to A)	
15)		A Plan, B) and C) Exposes: Ein Musikinstitut	1934
16)	Fragments:	A) The Conserver B) AS: Why no great American Music C) The same by Mr. Henderson D) Notes to A)	1934
17)		A) A Fragment: Casella, A Polemic (8) B) Rigoletto and Kammersymphony, an Analysis	??1936??

LIST TWO

MANUSCRIPTS, MOSTLY (REAL MANUSCRIPTS) HANDWRITTEN

SOME PERHAPS UNPUBLISHED
SOME FRAGMENTS

Ms	1	Concert Gebouw Jubiläum	1928
	2	Schreker's 50ter Geb.tag	1928
Ms	3a	Entwurf, 3b Reinschrift of "Vorwort zur Suite für Str. Orch (unveröffentlich{ })"	1935
"	4	Auskunft über das Streich-Quartett-Konzert	??1936??
Ms	5	Dankschreiben z/60ten-handschr	1934

Ms	6	Dr. D. J. Bach Briefentwurfe	
"	7	Akademie der Künste	
Ms	8	Preface and Introd of a counterp. textb.	1934
"	9	Musical idea (1st time in English)	1934
"	10	Outline to Verzierungen (see Theoretical 6)	1922
Ms	11	Manscr of an address in Chicago	1934
"	12	" " " " " New York (machine)	1933 the same
"	13	"_"_"_"_"_ _"_ _" (hand)	"
"	14	manuscr, address "Driven into the Paradise"	1934
"	15	" lecture USC What have people	?1935?36
"	16	" " Some objective reasons	XII, 1934
Ms	17a	Mechanische Musikinstrumente (Pult und Tst)	1926
"	17b	Walter Herbert Seligmans's Artikel	
"	18a	Ueber Klavierauszug: Entwurf, hand,	
"	18b	" " : article, masch	1923
19a, b,		Entwurf und Ausführung: Classes at USC	1935
Ms	20	Die heutige Situation der Musik	1929
Ms	21	Meine Meinung über Zeitgenössische Musik	1923
Ms	22	Interview mit mir selbst a) Reinschrift b) Konzept	1928
Ms	23a	Boheme (manuskript hand{)}	6.5.1928
"	23b	" Reinschrift (masch)	" " "

Appendix 4

A Comparison of Schoenberg's Lists and Rufer's Catalogue

The two columns below compare Rufer's and Schoenberg's lists of prose manuscripts. The comparison makes use of both Rufer's and Schoenberg's methods of labeling the same works. In his first main list (1932–40) Schoenberg assigns each manuscript to a subject category and identifies it by a number. His categories correspond to sections in Rufer's *Works of Arnold Schoenberg*. For example, Rufer's section D, "Music," includes all of Schoenberg's entries labeled "Musikalisches" or MUS. Also, Rufer's "Aesthetics," section E, corresponds to "Aesthetic" or KÜ; "My Theories," section F, to "Meine Theorien" or DEUT; "Monuments," section G, to "Denkmäler" or DENK; "Miscellaneous," section H, in part to "Vermischtes" or VERM; "Language," section J, to "Sprachliches" or SPR; "Ethics," section K, to "Moral" or MOR; and "Published Articles," section L, to "Gedruckte Aufsätze." Schoenberg's post-1940 "List of the Manuscripts" corresponds to Rufer's section C, "Articles, Essays." Schoenberg's list "Unfinished Theoretical Works" corresponds in part to Rufer's section C, "Articles and Essays," as well as to section A, "Theoretical Works." Items in Schoenberg's "*Manuscripts*, Mostly (Real Manuscripts) Handwritten, etc." appear in Rufer's section H, "Miscellaneous."

Abbreviations:

AN	Anekdoten
APH	Aphorismen
BIO	Biographisches
DENK	Denkmäler
KÜ	Kunst
MOR	Moral
MUS	Musikalisches
NAT	Natur
SPR	Sprachliches
VERM	Vermischtes

126 *Appendix 4*

Capital letters in the Rufer list correspond to the sections of Rufer's book discussed above.

Schoenberg *Rufer*

FIRST MAIN LIST

Abbreviated Topics and Manuscript Numbers:

AN 237c — omitted

APH 21–23, 33, 41, 43, 63, 71, 73, 83, 91, 96–97, 101, 111, 121, 125–26, 130, 150, 152, 161, 184, 211, 228, 229, 230, 237b, 241a–243, 248, 257–59, 300a, 316–18, 324–26, 329–33, 343, 365, 371, 378, 382, 384–86, 388, 392, 402–3, 406, 411, 423 — omitted

BIO 26, 50, 60, 74, 79, 82b, 84, 89, 92, 95, 100b, 108, 115, 124, 134–35, 149, 237a, 281, 285, 289, 295, 306, 319, 334, 350, 355–56, 361, 372, 379–81, 387, 391, 393, 396, 400, 405, 407, 408, 416–19, 425 — omitted

DENK 13, 15–16, 32, 48, 68, 82a, 87, 113, 118–19, 128, 133, 147–48, 179, 182–83, 184–85, 186–90, 192–94, 198–204, 229, 234–36a, 252, 266–67, 271, 279, 301, 307, 345–49, 353–54, 427 — exact except for omission of DENK 184–85, 229, 246: see section G, pp. 171–72

DEUT 25, 29, 52, 110, 116–17, 132, 141, 216–26, 244–45, 249, 260–62, 293, 344, 362–64, 377, 395, 397, 399, 413, 424 — exact except for omission of DEUT 25, 110, 116, 249: see section F, p. 170

KÜ 85, 127, 129, 151–53, 162–64, 167, 180–81, 208, 210, 278, 284, 292, 297b, 299b, 304, 313, 314, 320–21, 328, 336–37, 340 — exact except for omission of KÜ 152, 328: see section E, pp. 169–70

MOR 25, 77, 80, 93, 102, 168, 176–77a, 207, 231, 241b, 294, 303b, 359–60, 389, 294, 303b, 359, 389 — exact except for omission of MOR: see section K, pp. 175–76

MUS 1–7, 14, 18–20, 23–24, 27–28, 31, 34, 36–37, 40, 42, 45–47, 49, 51, 53–59, 61, 64–67, 69–70, 72, 75–76, 78a, 85–86, 88, 90, 94, 98–100a, 104–7, 109, 112, 114, 131, 136–40, — exact except for omission of MUS 54, 56: see section D, pp. 164–69

A Comparison of Schoenberg's Lists and Rufer's Catalogue

143–46, 154, 159–60, 165–66, 169–75, 177b, 191a, 195–97, 205–6, 273–77, 280, 287–88, 290–91, 297a–99, 302, 305, 308–10, 312, 315, 339–40, 351–52, 373–76, 383, 390, 394, 398, 401, 404, 409–10, 412, 415, 420–21, 426	
NAT 9, 238	omitted
SPR 8, 11–12, 30, 38, 78b, 103, 142, 209, 215, 322, 366–70	exact: see section J, pp.175
VERM 3, 17, 39, 44, 62, 81, 120, 122–23, 155–57, 178, 232–33, 239–40, 250, 253–54, 263–65, 268–70, 272, 282–83, 286, 300b, 303a, 323, 327, 338, 341–42, 357–58, 414, 422	exact except for omission of VERM 157, 300b, 358; an additional 37 entries labeled H-39–76 are added: see section H, pp.172–74
"LIST OF THE MANUSCRIPTS"	C-1–141, pp.156–60

"UNFINISHED THEORETICAL WORKS"

Nos.:

1	C-183, p.162
2	A-1a, p.135
3	A-3a–b, p.137
4	A-1b, p.135
5	A-1b, p.135
6	C-182, p.162
7	C-29, 30, p.157
8	A-2, pp.136–37
9	A-2, pp.136–37
10	A-2, pp.136–37
11	A-2, pp.136–37
12	C-151, p.161
13	C-154, p.161
14	C-181, p.162
15	C-174, p.161
16	C-184, p.162
17	C-175, p.161

"*MANUSCRIPTS*, MOSTLY (REAL MANUSCRIPTS) HANDWRITTEN, ETC."

Nos.

1	H-7, p.172

2	H-71, p.174
3	H-69, p.174
4	H-70, p.174
5	H-65, p.174
6	H-64, p.174
7	H-64, p.174
8	H-56, p.174
9	H-57, p.174
10	H-58, p.174
11	H-50, p.174
12	H-51, p.174
13	H-51, p.174
14	H-52, p.174
15	H-53, p.174
16	H-54, p.174
17a	H-60, p.174
17b	D-12, p.165
18a	H-61, p.174
18b	H-61, p.174
19	H-59, p.174
20	H-74, p.174
21	H-75, p.174
22	H-76, p.174
23a	H-66, p.174
23b	H-66, p.174
24	H-67, p.174
25	L-42, p.177
26	uncatalogued
27	H-72, p.174
28	H-73, p.174
29	uncatalogued
30	H-43, p.174
"GEDRUCKTE AUFSÄTZE" [PUBLISHED ARTICLES]	L-1-45

Appendix 5

A Comparison of Christensen and Christensen with Rufer and with Schoenberg

The following columns compare the catalogue of manuscripts compiled by the Christensens in *From Arnold Schoenberg's Literary Legacy* to Schoenberg's and Rufer's lists. The titles in the first column below correspond to sections of the Christensens' book. The roman numerals appearing under "Fragmente" and "Kleine Manuscripte" are subheadings within the same text. The manuscripts cited in the second and third columns are those that also appear in the Christensens' work. The capital letters in the third column correspond to the sections of Rufer's text: see Appendix 4.

CHRISTENSEN	SCHOENBERG	RUFER
"Anekdoten"	unlisted[1]	uncatalogued
"Dichtungen, Texte, Spruche, Aphorismen"	first main list: "Aphorismen" [APH]	uncatalogued
	"List of the Manuscripts," nos. 83, 85, 93	C-83, 85, 93, p.159
	"Gedruckte Aufsätze" [Published articles], nos. 9–11, 35	L-9, 11–24, p.176
	"List of Writings" APH. ANEK pp. 1–14[2]	uncatalogued
"Biographisches"	first main list	uncatalogued

---

1. Schoenberg's one entry under "Anekdoten" in the 1932–40 list, labeled *Zettel* — [Piece of paper —] [AN 237C], is uncatalogued in Christensen and Christensen.

2. The list is explained in Christensen and Christensen, *Literary Legacy*, 60.

"Fragmente"	"List of the Manuscripts," no.92	C-92, p.159
Specific References in "Fragmente":		
II-2	"List of the Manuscripts," no.80	C-80, p.158
III-1	unlisted	C-186, p.162
V-6	"List of the Manuscripts," no.124e	C-124e, p.159
"Glossen"	"List of the Manuscripts," no.77	C-77, p.158
"Jenseitiger Querkopf"	first main list, nos.88, 94, 98	D-42, 44, 45, p.166
	"Gedruckte Aufsätze," nos.41, 50	L-26, 27, p.177
"Kleine Manuscripte"		
I	"List of the Manuscripts," no.29	C-29, p.157
II	"List of the Manuscripts," no.30	C-30, p.157
III	unlisted	C-224, p.164
"Miscellaneous"	unlisted	uncatalogued
"Notebooks"	unlisted	uncatalogued
"Orchestration"	unlisted	A-4b, p.139; uncatalogued
"Sprachliches"	first main list, nos.215, 370	J-7, p.175; J-1, p.175

Works Cited

WORKS BY ARNOLD SCHOENBERG

Fundamentals of Musical Composition. Edited by Gerald Strang. New York: St. Martin's Press, 1967.

Letters. Edited by Erwin Stein and translated by Eithne Wilkins and Ernst Kaiser. New York: St. Martin's Press, 1965.

Models for Beginners in Composition. Edited by Leonard Stein. New York: G. Schirmer, 1943.

"Der musikalische Gedanke und seine Darstellung" (undated, notes dated 1929, 1940). Manuscript no.T37.4; T37.7–8, Arnold Schoenberg Institute, Los Angeles.

"Der musikalische Gedanke, seine Darstellung und Durchführung" (1925). Manuscript no.T37.4, T37.7–8. Arnold Schoenberg Institute, Los Angeles.

"Der musikalische Gedanke; seine Darstellung und Durchfuehrung" (undated). Manuscript no.T37.4–6. Arnold Schoenberg Institute, Los Angeles.

"Der musikalische Gedanke und die Logik, Technik und Kunst seine Darstellung" (1934–36). Manuscript no.T65.1–4. Arnold Schoenberg Institute, Los Angeles.

The Musical Idea and The Logic, Technique, and Art of Its Presentation by Arnold Schoenberg. Edited and translated by Patricia Carpenter and Severine Neff. New York: Columbia University Press, 1994.

Theory of Harmony. Translated by Roy E. Carter. Berkeley and Los Angeles: University of California Press, 1978.

Style and Idea. Edited by Leonard Stein. New York: St. Martin's Press, 1975.

SECONDARY SOURCES

Bailey, Walter, B. *Programmatic Elements in the Works of Schoenberg*. Ann Arbor, Mich.: UMI, 1984.

———. "Schoenberg's Published Articles: A List of Titles, Sources, and Translations." *Journal of the Arnold Schoenberg Institute* 4, no.2 (1980):156–61.

Carpenter, Patricia. "*Grundgestalt* as Tonal Function." *Music Theory Spectrum* 5 (1983): 15–38.

Christensen, Jean, and Jesper Christensen. *From Arnold Schoenberg's Literary Legacy: A Catalogue of Neglected Items*. Warren, Mich.: Harmonie Park Press, 1988.

Frisch, Walter. *Brahms and the Principle of Developing Variation*. Berkeley and Los Angeles: University of California Press, 1984.

Haimo, Ethan. *Schoenberg's Serial Odyssey: The Evolution of His Twelve-Tone Method, 1914–28*. Oxford: Clarendon Press, 1990.

Neff, Severine. "Schoenberg and Goethe: Organicism and Analysis." In *Music Theory and the Exploration of the Past*, edited by Christopher Hatch and David Bernstein. Chicago: University of Chicago Press, 1993.

Rufer, Josef. *The Works of Arnold Schoenberg*. Translated by Dika Newlin. London: Faber, 1962.

Simms, Bryan R. "Review of *Theory of Harmony* by Arnold Schoenberg, translated by Roy E. Carter." *Music Theory Spectrum* 4 (1982): 155–62.

Simpson, Reynold. "Archives Report: A Study of the U186 Sketches" (1990). Arnold Schoenberg Institute, Los Angeles. Photocopy.

———. "New Sketches, Old Fragments, and Schoenberg's Third String Quartet, Op.30." *Theory and Practice* 17 (1992).

Solie, Ruth A. "The Living Work: Organicism and Analysis." *Nineteenth-Century Music* 4, no.2 (1980): 147–56.

Stephan, Rudolf. "Schönbergs Entwurf über 'Das Komposition mit selbstständigen Stimmen.'" *Archiv für Musikwissenschaft* 29 (1972): 239–56.

Stuckenschmidt, H. H. *Schoenberg: His Life, Work, and World*. Translated by Humphrey Searle. New York: Schirmer Books, 1977.

Index

Aesthetic of Music (Schoenberg), xxiii, li
articulation: described, 23; and main and subordinate parts, 33–35

Babbitt, Milton, 1 n.33
Bach, J. S., 1 n.33, 5
Bailey, Walter B., xxxi n.21, lix n.55, 131
Beethoven: String Quartet op. 59, no. 1, 27; String Quartet op. 95, 89; Symphony no. 8, op. 93, 47
Bernstein, David W., liii n.44, 132
Brinkmann, Reinhold, xlvi n.30

cadence: and key, 45–47; and scale degrees, 49–51
Carpenter, Patricia, xxiv n.5, 131–32
Carter, Roy E., lvi n.49, 131
Christensen, Jean and Jesper: classification system on Schoenberg's works by, xxviii, xxxii; comparison between catalogues of Rufer/Schoenberg and, 129–30
coherence: principle of, 17; in art, 61–65; and comprehensibility, lxii, 9; and contrast, 21; described, 9; and developing variation, lxviii; and form, lvii–lxviii; and repetition, lxi, 37; theoretical works on, xxxiv; types of, 3–5, 61–63
Coherence (Schoenberg): outline for, 3–7, 11
Coherence, Counterpoint, Instrumentation, Instruction in Form: (*Zusammenhang, Kontrapunkt, Instrumentation, Formenlehre* [ZKIF]): and chronology of theoretical works, xxxiv–xxxviii; explanatory notes on text of, lxxi–lxxii; foreword of, 3; influence on Schoenberg's theoretical works, xxviii, xxviii–liii; and Rufer's catalogue, xxxii; transcription/translation of indexes for, 109–17
composition: unified theory of, lii, lxviii
compound forms, 103–5
comprehensibility: and coherence, lxii, 9, 19; and motive, lxiii, 25; and repetition, lxii; principles of, lxii–lxiii, 19, 23
contrast: and coherence, lxi, 21
counterpoint: theoretical works on, xxxiv–xxxv; exercise in, 69–71
Counterpoint [*Kontrapunkt*]: hexachordal sketches in, xxv

Der musikalische Gedanke, seine Darstellung und Durchführung [The musical idea, its presentation and development] (Schoenberg), lii
Der musikalische Gedanke und die Logik, Technik und Kunst seiner Darstellung [The musical idea and the logic, technique, and art of its presentation] (Schoenberg), xxiv, xxv, xxxiii
developing variation: described, lxiii–lxiv, lxviii, 39–43; in Mozart, String Quartet in C Major, K. 465, xxv, lxvi–lxviii. *See also* coherence, motive
Die Gesetze der musikalischen Komposition (Schoenberg), li
dissolution, 105

elaboration, 105
euphony, 97

filler voices, 65
form: and key, 47; manuscripts on, xxxvii; and meter, 55–59; organic, lvii–lviii; schoolbook-form, 35; and symmetry, 105; two- and three-part, 105
Frisch, Walter, lxiv n.63, 132
Fundamentals of Music Composition (Schoenberg), lxvi

Haimo, Ethan, xlii, xlv n.30, xlvii n.31, 1 n.33, 132
Harmonielehre [*Theory of Harmony*] (Schoenberg), xxiii, xxv, lvi, lii, lviii
Hatch, Christopher, liii n.44, 132
Hertzka, Emil, xxiii
hexachordal sketches in *Counterpoint:* described, xlii–v, 70–74; historical significance of, xxxiii, xlvii; Variations for Orchestra, and op. 31, xlvi–l

I-H combination, xlii–xliii
independent voice, 65–67
Instruction in Form (Schoenberg): outline for, 103–7
Instruction in Instrumentation (Schoenberg): exercise book for, 101; outline for, 77–85; piano arrangements in, 97–99
instrumentation: capabilities and character of instruments, 84–97; and composition, 79–81; theoretical works on, xxxvi–xxxviii; transposing instruments, 99–101

Kaiser, Ernst, xxiv n.3
Kandinsky, Wassily, li n.37
key: and cadence, 47, 49–55; and form, 47

liquidation, 39
Luginbühl, Anita, lxxi n.66

McBride, Jerry, xxx
melodic voice, 67–69
motive: and comprehensibility, lxiii, 25; described, lxiii–lxiv, 25–31; and repetition, 37–39. *See also* developing variation, repetition

Mozart: String Quartet in C Major, K. 465, xxv, xxxiii, liii, lxviii, 41–43
music theory: and organicism, liii–lvii; and Schoenberg, liii–lvii; unified theory of composition and, lii
musical idea (*Gedanke*): and coherence, 17–19, 61–63; manuscripts on, lii, xxxviii–ix; presentation of, 105; and unified theory of composition, lii
musical idea (*Idee*), 5
musical joining, 11
musical logic, 5–7

Neff, Severine, xxiv n.5, liii n.44, 131–32
Newlin, Dika, 132

orchestration. *See* instrumentation
organicism, liii–lvii. *See also* form, music theory

Plotinus (Roman philosopher), lv

rearrangement, xliii, xlv
recitatives, 107
repetition: and coherence, lxi; and comprehensibility, lxii, 105; and motive, lxiii, 31, 37; and rhythm, 31–33, 59; and variation, 21
rhythm: described, 31–33; and duration, 11, and meter, 55–59
ripieno voices, 65
Rufer, Josef: classification system on Schoenberg's works by, xxviii, xxxii; comparison between catalogues of Christensen/Schoenberg and, 129–30; comparison between Schoenberg's list and catalogue of, 125–28

Schoenberg, Arnold: bibliographic lists compiled by, 121–23; comparison between catalogues of Christensen/Schoenberg and, 129–30; comparison between Rufer's catalogue and list of, 125–28; and music theory, liii–lvii; influence of ZKIF on theoretical works of, xxviii–liii; plans for a unified theory of composition by, xxiii–xxv, li–liii; and theory of perception, lix–lxiii; transcription/translation of indexes by, 109–17; twelve-tone method of, xxv, xli, lii; *works cited: Die glückliche Hand,* 35; *Die Jakobsleiter,* xxv; String Quartet No. 1, op. 7, xxxi; Variations for Orchestra, op. 31, xxv, xlvi–l

Schwarzwald, Eugenie, xxiv

Searle, Humphrey, xxiv n.3, 132

Shoaf, R. Wayne, xxviii, xxx

similarity: described, 11; and understanding, 11–15

Simms, Bryan R., xxiii n.2, 132

Simpson, Reynold, xlix n.32, 132

Solie, Ruth A., liii n.44, 132

Stein, Erwin, xxiv n.3, 131

Stein, Leonard, xxiv n.5, xli n., 131

Stephan, Rudolf, xxiii n.1, 132

Steuermann, Clara, xxx

Strang, Gerald, xxiv n.7, 131

structure: principles of, 37

Stuckenschmidt, H. H., 132

symmetry: and inversion, 61; and form, 105

theme, 35

Theory of Composition ["Kompositionslehre"] (Schoenberg): chronology of xxxviii–xli; and "idea" manuscripts, xxiii, lii

Theory of Musical Coherence ["Lehre vom musikalischen Zusammenhang"] (Schoenberg), li

tonality, 47

transition: described, lxvi; in Mozart, String Quartet in C Major, K. 465, lxvi–lxviii

twelve-tone method: I-H combination, xlii–xliii; theoretical works on, xli. *See also* hexachordal sketches in *Counterpoint*

understanding: described, lix–x; and similarity, 11–15; and listening, lix; versus comprehensibility, lix

unified theory of composition, lii, lxviii–lxix

unraveling, 39

variation: lxi, 21. *See also* developing variation, repetition

Wilkins, Eithne, xxiv n.3, 131

Zehme, Albertine, xxiv n.3